# CATHOLICS COURAGEOUS

# CATHOLICS COURAGEOUS

## ALFRED K. ALLAN

FOREWORD BY RICHARD CARDINAL CUSHING

THE CITADEL PRESS    NEW YORK

# Foreword

As old, at least as the Gospels themselves is the story-telling device known as the parable, the "human-interest story" that partially veils a moral or religious truth. Through this means, the world's greatest narrators have caught our interest on two levels: on the level of sheer narrative, and on the level of instruction, of teaching the truth indirectly.

This readable, highly interesting, and informative collection of pieces is true to the parable form in all but one respect—there is no element of fiction here; each of the score of stories is a true story, a profile in Catholic courage that should appeal to everyone and instruct the majority on what it means to be self-sacrificing, charitable, courteous, faith-full, patriotic, and otherwise Christian in the basic meaning of that meaningful term.

The author's tales are drawn from life. They tell the stories of dramatists and barbers, members of labor unions and of Serra International, of speech therapists, social workers, nurses, boxers, and nuns. No one of the chapters is less than interesting, and all have that subsurface level of instruction with the power to make saints of us all.

Many of the names on parade here are familiar: Bing Crosby, Father Peyton, Dr. Tom Dooley, Father Flanagan of Boys Town, Boston's own Father Dan McColgan. Others are less familiar, but their stories also deserve telling, and *Catholics Courageous* has told them all well.

I unhesitatingly recommend the book to everyone.

Richard Cardinal Cushing
Archbishop of Boston

# Contents

# ACKNOWLEDGMENTS

"Adelaide Helps Change the World" and "The Greatest Crusade of Its Kind" originally appeared in *Mary Immaculate*. "The Barber and the Orphans" originally appeared in *The Holy Name Journal*. A condensed version of this article also appeared in *Catholic Digest*. "Operation Christmas" originally appeared in *Catholic Life*. "Saint Bruno in the Slums" originally appeared in *Our Lady of the Sacred Heart*. "Mom Levy and St. Joseph" originally appeared in *St. Anthony's Messenger*. "Courage in a Wheelchair" originally appeared in *Family Digest*. "Faith Behind the Footlights" originally appeared in *The Magnificat*. "Courageous Convert Makers" and "The Boxing Champ Who Became an Altar Boy" originally appeared in *The Apostle*. "Young Drug Addicts Are His Friends" originally appeared in *Extension*. "The Miracle Man of Speech Afflictions" and "Troubadours of Mary" originally appeared in *The Victorian*. "Wheels for Our Lady" originally appeared in *Today's Family*. "How Bill Gargan Licked Cancer," "Jerry Walsh Walks Again," and a shorter version of "They're Keeping Tom Dooley's Promises" originally appeared in *The Catholic Layman*. A condensed version of "Jerry Walsh Walks Again" appeared in *Catholic Digest*. Shorter versions of "Where Labor and Management Meet," "The Courageous Young Men of ACTU," and "To Fill the Church's Greatest Need" originally appeared in *Our Sunday Visitor*. "Dick Rendich's Modern Crusade," "Neighbors Get Together," and "Dedicated Dramatist" originally appeared in *The Eucharist*. "Centers For The Salvage of Human Beings" and "Frank Smith—Racketbuster" originally appeared in *U.S. Catholic*. A condensed version of "Troubadours of Mary" also was published in *Family Digest*. Condensed versions of "The Greatest Crusade of Its Kind," "Where Labor and Management Meet," "St. Bruno in the Slums," "Faith Behind the Footlights," "The Boxing Champ Who Became an Altar Boy," "How Bill Gargan Licked Cancer," and "Young Drug Addicts Are His Friends" also appeared in *Irish Digest*. "Dolores Hart: From Stardom to Convent" appeared originally in *Our Sunday Visitor*. The author wishes to express his gratitude to all of the above publications for granting him permission to use this material in this book.

# Introduction

One afternoon a few years ago I was at work in my office when I received a phone call from a good friend of mine, Joe Spagnola of Mary Productions. "Al, I have to tell you about a very remarkable woman I've just had the privilege of meeting," Joe said with great enthusiasm. "Her name is Mary Varick. She had been a victim of both polio and cancer, yet she is now leading a normal, useful life and is an exemplary mother and wife. You *must* write a story on her. She can be an inspiration to hundreds."

I did write Mary Varick's story, and a short while later it was published in *The Family Digest*. Soon after it appeared, Mary and I were literally snowed under with letters and phone calls from people who had read the story and who just had to tell us how much it had moved and uplifted them.

I reflected for awhile on this result of my writing effort. If this story of the courage and faith of just one Catholic woman could have such a profound effect on other people, I thought, how much more good could be accomplished by telling the stories of other courageous Catholic men and women.

This idea impelled me to begin what would be several years of often exhausting but always spiritually rewarding ' work, seeking out such inspiring accounts of the power of faith and courage. My journeys would take me to many cities in different parts of the country and put me in the friendly company of many interesting people. I would meet Bill Gargan, the veteran motion picture actor who had successfully fought against a dread disease and was now using this added time God had given him on earth to help others facing the same serious problem. There was Joe Pestana, a humble barber who had been raised in an orphanage and is today spending much of his time in an unselfish personal mission to make the lives of orphan children fuller and happier. Then there was Tommy Loughran, the one-time world's light-heavyweight boxing champion, who is saving scores of young boys from becoming juvenile delinquents by guiding them into useful and productive channels of youthful activity. And the Spagnola family, people of only modest means who, at their own expense and without thought to financial gain, tour the country performing their own plays and skits on religious themes before enthusiastic audiences, thereby bringing the truths of the Catholic faith to millions.

My journeys would also enable me to learn about and record the dedicated work being done by the priests and lay members of such important Catholic organizations as the Association of Catholic Trade Unionists, the Family Rosary Crusade, Wheels for Our Lady, the Blackfriars Guild, the Family Communion Crusade, and numerous others.

I would meet people from all walks of life, all of them sharing two things in common: an unswering devotion to their Faith which is a vital factor in all they do and a sincerely-felt modesty about their accomplishments. Many, in fact, were reluctant at first to speak about themselves for fear others would think they were seeking personal glory or some special recognition for their deeds of courage and self-sacrifice. They finally agreed to tell their stories in the hope that their experiences would be a source of inspiration to others. It is these stories that form the basis of this book.

There are many people who made this book possible. This is by way of expressing my gratitude to all of them. To Christine Dunst for constantly encouraging me to keep writing during the tough early years. To all of the people I have written about in this book for cooperating with me and for allowing me to tell their stories. To the editors of the Catholic magazines in which these stories originally appeared for granting me permission to gather them together in this permanent form.

Finally, I believe I can best sum up the overall purpose of this book by quoting from a passage in the late John F. Kennedy's book, *Profiles in Courage:*

"The stories of past courage can teach, they can offer hope, they can provide inspiration. But they can't supply courage itself. For this each man must look into his own soul."

ALFRED K. ALLAN

*New York City*

*CATHOLICS COURAGEOUS*

# Operation Christmas

THE BIG SIGN on the porch of the good-sized, white-frame Demchak home off 133rd Street in Queens, New York, reads simply, "Keep Christ in Christmas." A brace of holiday lights surrounds the sign, making it visible for some distance.

On a bright December day, a visitor rings the front bell and is received at the door by the friendly smile of the man of the house, Leonard Demchak. Leonard is forty-five years old, rather tall, boyish-faced. He's a dedicated Catholic Actionist who is personally conducting his own campaign to restore the proper meaning to the Christmas celebration. It is this story that the visitor has come to hear.

He walks with Leonard into the neatly kept living room and is made immediately aware of the religious spirit that permeates this comfortable home. Some three hundred religious ornaments and decorations are set about the rooms. A Christmas tree adorns one side of the living room, and placed beneath it is an elaborate display that Leonard fashioned himself illustrating the Christmas story and the five joyful mysteries of the Rosary.

Seated around the display is the Demchak family, Leonard's

wife, Pearl, his two young sons, Thomas and Leonard, Jr., and his eighteen-year-old daughter, Georgine. The visitor starts by asking Leonard the question that is most on his mind: "Why do you have such an overpowering interest in the Christmas season?"

"I guess I've always loved Christmas," Lenny replies thoughtfully.

As a boy in the small, closely knit town of Askam, Pennsylvania, he'd always known the beautiful, old-fashioned Christmas that was so much a part of his Polish ancestry. At the Christmas Eve dinner there would be the prayers before and after the meal and the sharing of the blessed unleavened bread that represented Christ and that had been prepared at the church for just this special occasion. Then the placing of the crèche, or crib, under the just decorated Christmas tree, followed by the older members of the family leaving for midnight mass. In the morning the youngsters would rise early, come down the stairs to see the Christmas tree and, before anything else, to pay their respects to the figure of the Christ Child in the crib.

"It was a time of great thanksgiving, not just of gift-giving," Lenny recalls. "It gave all of us a feeling of pride and peace." This custom is still observed in Lenny's home today.

On Christmas Eve, 1944, Lenny was serving in the United States Army in the faraway Aleutian Islands. A raging blizzard had left the island covered by deep banks of clean, white snow. A heavy truck jogged into the camp and a good number of the men piled in. The truck was taking them to the midnight mass being conducted some distance away. Lenny had been on outpost duty near the camp and had not gotten back until eleven o'clock. "The truck just left, you missed it," one of his buddies told him as he walked into camp. "I don't want to miss the Christmas Mass," Lenny thought to himself. He started out across the snow, slogging through the ankle-deep drifts,

Mrs. Pearl Demchak with sons Thomas and Leonard
John Jr. at their backyard shrine.

Leonard John Demchak before one of his Christmas posters.

the cold wind tearing at his face. The snow shone a glistening white in the glare of the full moon. It was a ten-mile hike to the service but Lenny was determined to make it.

"As I walked I thought of the Wise Men traveling on just such a night to the crib of the Christ Child. The heavens seemed to be opening up above me, guiding me on my journey. It was the most beautiful night I could remember."

These moments of Christmas inspiration from his childhood and manhood stayed in Lenny's mind. He was discharged from the service in 1945, got married, obtained a job as a guard for a Wall Street bank, and became active in Catholic Action work at St. Teresa of Avila Church in Richmond Hill, New York.

"Let me make it clear that I'm not against gift giving at Christmas time," Lenny told me. "Gift giving has its rightful place in the celebration but it seems to me that, despite all the tinsel and pomp that we see in the department stores around Christmas time we are still overlooking the true meaning of the holiday we are celebrating."

To harness action to his thoughts Lenny embarked in full earnest on what he called his "Operation Christmas." As the first step he had made up at his own expense some five thousand buttons and signs bearing the message "Keep Christ in Christmas" and had them distributed to public and parochial schools and Catholic organizations.

Next, he drew up what he called "The Wisdom of Washington"—a handsome scroll on which was printed some excerpts from the writings and diaries of our first President, in which George Washington affirmed his belief in God and his reliance on spiritual values. These scrolls were also widely distributed and would be useful not only at Christmas time but also all year round.

Then a shocking situation came to Lenny's attention. The country was being flooded by Christmas cards that flagrantly

Georgine Demchak and the family's Nativity display.

mocked the meaning of the holiday. Lenny quickly dispatched a letter of protest to a local newspaper. "The very principles of decency are being undermined by these crude, salacious, and repugnant cards," he wrote with sincere indignation, urging a clean-up. He also arranged a meeting with representatives of the Greeting Card Association, an organization of leading greeting card publishers, and obtained from them their whole-hearted support of his campaign. Several local newspapers backed him up with strong editorials condemning the offensive greeting cards.

At just about that time the New York State legislature was drawing up a bill aimed at stopping the increasing flood of obscene literature. The legislators, heeding this wave of protest started by Lenny, added a provision to their new bill providing stiff penalties for the manufacture and distribution of offensive Christmas cards. Thanks to Lenny's campaign, this form of irreverence toward Christmas has been eliminated.

"Operation Christmas" is now a regular year-end project for Lenny. Using his own money and the contributions he receives from individuals and organizations, Lenny has posted billboards in his neighborhood proclaiming his "Keep Christ in Christmas" message, and he distributes specially designed Nativity cards which urge the recipients to remember the true meaning of the holiday. (Nearly thirty thousand Nativity cards were distributed by Lenny last Christmas.)

He has also had a series of slides made bearing his Christmas message and has had them flashed during the holiday season on television programs that cover some twenty states. As Lenny says, "Christmas, like life, is empty without Christ."

The visitor now has his story of one man's special devotion to the Christmas celebration. It is a devotion shared equally by his entire family, in particular by his wife, Pearl, who has stayed up through many a night with him as he pores over new campaign ideas. "How do you like this one?" he'll ask her, his papers, filled with suggestions, spread out on the kitchen table. He is convinced that "if Pearl likes the idea it's sure to be good."

Only one other thing now needs to be seen—the religious shrine in the backyard of the Demchak home. Lenny escorts the visitor outside into the cold, winter freshness. The shrine is set back at the end of the good-sized yard, looking out toward the house. An oval arch covers a statue of the Blessed Mother which stands over the figure of the Christ Child asleep in a wooden crib filled with hay. Outlining the open arch are a number of Christmas lights. Snow has just fallen and flakes are now heaped around the arch. A thin film of snow covers the lights, but doesn't shut them out entirely. Instead, a blue haze manages to filter through, surrounding the figures with a strange, heavenly glow.

The visitor stands in awe at this sight. It is the peacefulness and beauty of the Christmas season that Lenny has been speaking of. No further words need be said now, except perhaps Lenny's own softly spoken declaration, "I'll always love Christmas."

Here are some suggestions from Leonard Demchak on how you can launch your own Operation Christmas:

*As an individual*: Do something to actively support the idea, within your own family, circle of friends and business contacts:

1. Have a Christmas display inside your home or outdoors.
2. Make a Christ Crib as a family project.
3. Urge your friends and neighbors to use similar displays.
4. Tell the story of the Christ Child to your children so they will understand the true meaning of Christmas.
5. Attend Christmas church services.
6. Select Christmas cards with a spiritual significance.
7. Use Christmas seals containing the Nativity scene.

*As a member of a club, association, or church group:*

1. Help organize the membership's observance of the Christmas season to reflect the holy spirit of the occasion.
2. Initiate some specific Christmas program to tie in with the community campaign.

*As an educator or leader of youth groups:*

1. Organize such activities as the building of Nativity scenes for indoor home use or for outdoor display.
2. See that the children or young people in these groups are made aware of the true meaning of Christmas by telling the story of the first Christmas and what it meant to the world.

*As a business or professional person:*

1. Put a Christmas Crib scene in your display window, reception room, or outside your plant or place of business.
2. Display "Christmas, Like Life, is Empty Without Christ" posters.
3. Utilize your billboard (large and small), bus, and streetcar advertising space during December for the "Keep Christ in Christmas" message.
4. Use newspaper advertising with appropriate art work (the Nativity scene, etc.) and copy.

II

# Courage in a Wheelchair

MARY VARICK, a cheerful-faced, hearty and happy woman in her late forties, boasts proudly of being a member of Christ's "inner circle" of the handicapped and the afflicted. Mary has been crippled since childhood and soon she will also be blind, yet this courageous and amazing mother of four fine children considers her serious afflictions as "God's greatest gift to me!"

Mary Varick has not only accepted her afflictions with grace; she has also devoted her life to helping other handicapped people discover the happiness and contentment she herself has found.

When Mary was but eighteen months old she was stricken with crippling polio which left both her legs paralyzed. Her parents faced their child's sudden affliction bravely, believing firmly that God must have had His reason for making their child so different from other children.

The family often visited Philadelphia, where Mary's mother had been born; there the little crippled child would be carried into beautiful St. Anne's Church in her mother's arms. Mary's mother would hold her close to her, then she would kneel down and say over and over, "Oh Good Saint Anne, pray for me."

Mary grew to womanhood in the modest but comfortable home her family owned on a quiet street in Jersey City, New Jersey. Though she always had to use crutches she attended the local public school, from which she was graduated in the year 1929.

That summer after graduation Mary met a handsome, gangling young man, Bill Varick. Bill would see Mary sitting on the porch of her parents' home and he would stop to say hello and engage her in conversation. Bill told his friends that he couldn't go past Mary's house without speaking to the "laughing pretty girl who is crippled."

Bill was an athlete and a mighty good dancer; yet he spent most of his time sitting beside Mary and talking with her instead of dating other girls in the neighborhood. Sometimes they would go for a walk, Mary hobbling along on her crutches, Bill walking devotedly beside her, two very happy people very much in love.

Then the summer came to an end. Bill hadn't called her or come to visit her for several days. Perhaps he has decided that it is better if we no longer see each other, Mary thought, fearful that her serious affliction had finally forced Bill to reconsider his feelings for her. Then, shortly after Labor Day, Bill phoned her. His voice was tense and urgent. "Would you go for a ride with me? I have something to say to you, Mary."

An hour later they were settled in Bill's car, moving slowly down a little country road. Bill had been silent for several minutes, but now he finally spoke what was on his mind. "I find life very dull without you," he confessed, "and it annoys me to find that most girls live in a dull little world of dates and dances and dresses. I want to marry you, Mary."

Mary excitedly caught her breath as Bill continued:

"I never gave a thought to God's universe until I watched the moon come up with you, and found that you knew almost every star by name. You've got a kind of beauty and under-

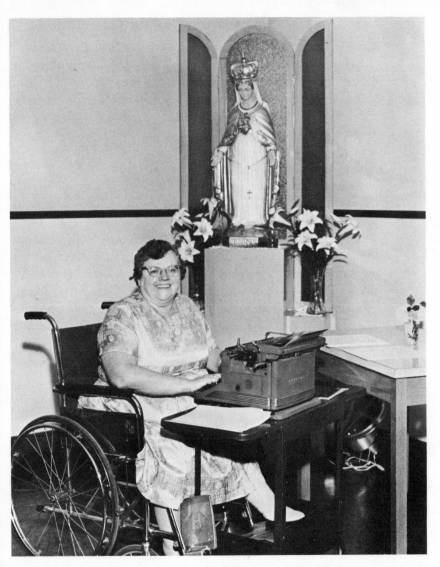

Mary Varick at work on her **second book.**

standing I've never known, and I want to share it with you."

Mary was deeply in love with Bill but she now wondered if it was right for her to burden him all his life, caring for a "cripple." They talked it over for nearly an hour before they came to a decision. "We will make a novena to the Sacred Heart for guidance. Perhaps then we will know if our marriage would be right."

For nine nights Mary and Bill fervently prayed. Then, their novenas ended, they sat together in the dining room of Mary's home, hoping for some sign that would show them the right path to take.

Suddenly the front door was opened wide and Mary's mother came in. She was carrying a package in her hand which turned out to be a beautiful home-blessing of the Sacred Heart. "All this week, I've had the funniest feeling that some day, Mary, you'll have a home all your own and I wanted to be the first to give you a gift for that home," Mary's mother said. Bill and Mary looked at each other. "What more eloquent answer could you want, Mary dear?" Bill said, on the verge of joyful tears. "Yes," Mary answered, "our marriage will be right."

On June 4, 1937, on the Feast of the Sacred Heart, Mary, as difficult as it was, walked on crutches down the aisle of All-Saints Church in Jersey City. Her face shone with happiness as she rested her hand on the arm of her beloved Bill. They were united in a glorious nuptial mass and immediately afterwards Bill said, "I'm sure our marriage will work, Mary, because it's built on the firm foundation of love, respect, and understanding." They couldn't then know of the many tests of strength to which their love would be put in the years to follow.

On September 17, 1938, they were blessed with their first child, a daughter, christened Wilma Mary but affectionately called "Billie." The Varick family was now starting to grow, so Bill and Mary decided to pool what financial resources ·they had and buy a home in the suburbs of Jersey City. It was in this neatly kept dwelling that their second child, James, was born. Here too Mary bore two more daughters, Barbara and Mary. The Varicks were truly rich in God's blessings, until one fateful day in 1949.

Mary began to experience severe pains in her legs. A thorough medical check-up revealed the worst: she had cancer. The doctors believed that it was hopeless. They said she had only a short time to live.

Mary broke the bad news to Bill and the children and asked them to have courage. "God only asks great sacrifices of the ones He loves the most," she explained to them, for Mary had no fear of death. "God has given me a greater reward than I could ever have dreamed of. He gave me Daddy and you children."

And Bill, fighting back his tears, added, "God will see us through."

The family was plunged into serious debt to pay Mary's hospital and medical bills. Nevertheless, they had a Christmas celebration that year and the Varick home remained a bright and happy place.

Shortly afterwards Mary made a request of Bill. "Will you take me to the Shrine of Ste. Anne de Beaupré in Canada? I remember my mother praying to Saint Anne when we visited the church in Philadelphia and I have something I want to ask at the Shrine."

Bill knew that such a long trip would be difficult and painful for his Mary but he was determined to fulfill what might well be his wife's last wish.

Mary's brother Edward helped them reach the quaint little French-Canadian village that held the world-famous shrine. They arrived on a pleasantly warm July seventeenth in 1951. The Shrine stood atop a hillside; below it rolled the calm waters of the Saint Lawrence River. Tears of great joy were in Mary's eyes as, in her wheelchair, she was taken into the Shrine's magnificent church. And during Communion, Mary whispered the wish that had brought her on this brave journey: "O my Jesus, you know I have never minded being crippled, and that I willingly offered this affliction to You every day, in thanksgiving for the many blessings You have given me. But now I beg You to let me stay with my family and be of some help to them." Even at this moment, when death seemed very near, Mary was not thinking of herself, but only of her Bill and their children.

Bill noticed afterwards that Mary was smiling contentedly. He couldn't know then why Mary now seemed so joyfully happy for she hadn't told Bill what her wish had been.

That evening, during Benediction, Mary was inside the glorious Basilica of the Shrine, silently praying to Saint Anne, as her mother had done many years before in Philadelphia. Suddenly, as she opened her eyes, Mary realized that something unbelievable had happened: She was no longer in her wheelchair. Somehow, though she could never explain it, she was now kneeling alone at the foot of the Miraculous Statue of Good Saint Anne.

When she and Bill returned home, Mary had another thorough examination. Something miraculous had indeed taken place. All traces of her cancer had disappeared, never to return again.

Exalted by the new lease on life that had been given her, Mary made a sacred vow: "I will return each year to the Shrine with my family and friends, in gratitude for her goodness to me." It was a vow Mary meant to keep, no matter how difficult this would be.

She spent the next several months in feverish activity organizing her first pilgrimage to the Shrine. Railroads had to be contacted, hotel accommodations for her family and friends had to be arranged. One by one, prospective pilgrims called her

Mary Varick and one of her pilgrimage groups.

to indicate their heartfelt desire to be part of her new "journey of life" to the Shrine. Mary and Bill had to renew the mortgage on their home to cover their expenses for the trip, but they did so gladly.

On July 15, 1952, the Varick family, Mary, Bill and the children, and some thirty-seven other pilgrims, arrived at the Shrine after a long and arduous trip. The difficulties of traveling were now forgotten. Here at the Shrine the pilgrims found the spiritual rewards that make all labors worthwhile.

For Mary, this was only the beginning. No sooner was she home from this pilgrimage than she began to marshal her forces for another pilgrimage that year. Often, even up to the last minute, she didn't know if she would have enough money to pay for the trip, but somehow the needed funds, and help in other ways, always came through just in time. The pilgrims had made plans to visit the Shrine of Our Lady of the Cape, situated halfway between Montreal and Ste. Anne de Beaupré. But they had not yet been able to arrange suitable transportation for the journey. They were supposed to depart in just a few weeks, and still no means of travel had been found. Would this trip, which meant so much to the pilgrims, have to be called off?

"My faith in God and Good Saint Anne remained strong. I couldn't give up," Mary now recalls. The answer to her prayers came with the ringing of the phone in her house. A good friend of hers was calling to offer his car for the trip.

Each time Mary planned a new pilgrimage her group of pilgrims grew in numbers. Finally she realized that the most feasible thing to do was to charter a bus for her group. Bill, who now worked for the Public Service bus line, would drive, donating his salary to pay the way for some pilgrim who otherwise couldn't afford to go. The bus held forty passengers and Mary had to fill every seat, or she and Bill would have the added financial burden of having to pay for the empty seats.

Mary again prayed for help. "I begged the Sacred Heart not to let this first bus pilgrimage fail," she now reminisces.

The next day Mary's phone never stopped ringing. It suddenly seemed as though everyone was calling her to make reservations for the pilgrimage, though until then only a very few had telephoned. Reluctantly she had to turn away six people since there was no room for them in the bus!

Mary recalls the beautiful twenty-year-old girl who had been crippled by polio. The girl had always wanted to be a model but now, of course, this was impossible. Her parents had prayed for her, but when their prayers didn't seem to be answered they turned against religion itself, scorning it bitterly and refusing to go to the sacraments. When their young daughter decided she wanted to join Mary's first bus pilgrimage, both parents objected strongly, but finally, realizing how determined she was to make the trip, they decided to go with her. "But we're only going along to take care of our daughter. We no longer believe in the power of prayer," they insisted to Mary.

During the ride up to the Shrine, Mary engaged the girl's mother in long, friendly conversations. "Did you ever think that your daughter's affliction proves that God loves her far more than you do?" Mary asked. The mother was startled by such an idea. Mary then explained: "Since a modeling career could quite easily have involved her in so much worldly success and pleasure that she might have forgotten God and completely lost her soul, this cross she carries may easily have been His way of assuring her eternal happiness, instead of granting her a few fleeting years of worldly joy."

The mother and father pondered Mary's words deeply. Will they see how wrong their attitude is? Mary wondered hopefully.

At the Shrine, the parents, tearful and overcome with emotion, watched as their daughter courageously climbed the Scala Sancta (Holy Stairs) leading to the glorious place of religious devotion. Suddenly the mother fell to her knees and began to climb the stairs behind her daughter. A little while later both parents went to confession and received their first Holy Communion after so many years, affirming their spiritual rebirth.

On May 31, 1958, the Feast of the Queenship of Mary, the Varnicks had their own personal moment of joy when Billie, their eldest daughter, was married, and at the same altar and by the same priest who had united Bill and Mary in their miraculous marriage.

On the first Saturday in March, 1959, Mary undertook her most important mission for the Shrine of Ste. Anne de Beaupré. She had learned that regular travel tours did not take seriously afflicted pilgrims because they feared that the trip would be too difficult for them. "But they are the ones who *most* need to visit the Shrines," Mary insisted, and that day she made a vow: "If God will give me the strength and ability to do so, I am going to organize a pilgrimage just for the seriously handicapped, and I'm going to find a way to raise funds to bring along those who are unable to pay their own way!"

Months of purposeful struggle and sacrifice followed. Mary and Bill had to sign a second mortgage on their home to raise enough money to cover at least the initial expenses for the big pilgrimage. But Mary was determined that this great task she had set for herself would be accomplished. A number of her friends formed a "First Saturday Club" to raise money for Mary's pilgrimage, and they also began to take the seriously handicapped to mass, confession, and Communion at least once a month as their way of fulfilling Our Lady's Fátima request regarding the first Saturday of each month. The club held dozens of raffles, card parties, drawings, auctions—anything that could bring them in some funds.

It was about this time that Mary learned that she had a

disease of the cornea, one that will eventually lead to total blindness. Yet this knowledge did not stop her from fulfilling her vow to the other members of what she has called "Christ's inner circle of the handicapped and afflicted."

There was a year of painstaking effort and many new setbacks and discouragements to be overcome by Mary and her friends. But they kept on. "We had a little boy with multiple sclerosis, a paraplegic veteran, a priest who had been very badly disfigured in a laboratory blast, a blind nun, and a seriously ill Negro girl, and we just couldn't let them down. They had to have their 'vacation with God' no matter what the cost," Mary says, affirming the faith and iron-willed determination of her First Saturday Club members.

Finally, on August 15, the great pilgrimage of the lame and the sick began their wearisome but magnificent journey. The nonhandicapped volunteer helpers who went along gently helped the pilgrims on and off the trains and buses, and at last they arrived at the sacred Shrine for the most exalting moments of their lives.

It is interesting to note that Mary doesn't restrict any of her pilgrimage groups to Catholics. People of other faiths are also welcome, so strong is Mary's belief that we are all "God's children."

There was the young Protestant woman who phoned Mary one afternoon. "I walk with crutches. I don't believe that you take non-Catholics on your pilgrimages or that you take people· who can't pay," the woman said sharply. Mary was then organizing a shorter trip to the National Shrine of the Immaculate Conception in Washington D.C. She perceived, from the antagonistic tone of the caller's voice, that here was a woman whose severe affliction had embittered her and made her suspicious of others. "You are welcome to come with us no matter what your faith is, and if you are unable to pay your own way we will pay for you," Mary said cordially. When

Mary told the other members of her group how rudely the woman had spoken, they said that perhaps she shouldn't be taken along. But Mary answered, "This woman is very unhappy. She needs us."

On the way to the nation's capital the woman continued to act belligerently. But Mary tried to win her friendship. She told her of her own trouble-beset life and how, despite everything, she was a happy, contented woman and mother. One of the nonhandicapped volunteer helpers, a young Catholic man, also made friends with her. By the time they reached Washington the woman was more relaxed and cordial toward the others in the group.

Almost from the moment the woman first saw the great Shrine she began to reconsider her previous narrow outlook. She thought again of Mary and how this brave woman had learned to live with her affliction without foolish self-pity or bitterness. She was now feeling deeply the power of the Shrine.

A few months after the group had returned home Mary learned that the woman and the young Catholic man who had befriended her were soon to be married. They were wed at a Mass and shortly afterwards the woman was converted to the Catholic faith. The young couple's first child was named Edna Mary after the woman who had helped to change its mother's life, as she has changed the lives of so many others through her inspiring example.

Mary Varick continues to plan new pilgrimages. So far she has organized over fifteen trips to various shrines in the United States and Canada. And she is determined to continue her work even after blindness eventually overcomes her. She also speaks frequently before religious and civic organizations, and she recently made a recording of her voice as she repeated the Meditations of the Way to the Cross; all proceeds from the record's sale are donated to the Madonna House for pilgrims and invalids at the Our Lady of the Cape Shrine in Quebec,

Canada. Through the years she has seen her own wonderful family grow, sturdy in body and spirit. Mary and Bill now live with their married daughter at 51 Clifton Avenue in Newark, New Jersey.

It is Mary Varick's dream to see that every invalid, no matter how serious their affliction or how low their financial status, is able to visit a shrine. Those who are privileged to know this graciously cheerful and courageous woman are sure that because of her unswerving faith her dream will come true.

# III

# The Barber and the Orphans

THE GLITTERING ballroom of the Hotel Stacey in Trenton, New Jersey, was jammed to capacity. The annual dinner of the local chapter of the Junior Chamber of Commerce (Jaycee) was in progress. The audience was quiet and attentive as Harold N. Scherer, the chapter's president, announced the names of the five New Jersey men whom the organization had chosen as the most outstanding young men in the state.

Joe Pestana, one of the invited guests, leaned forward nervously in his chair. Joe, thirty-nine years old, rather tall, and of moderate build, is a local barber. Sitting nearby was his attractive, dark-haired wife, Ann, who had persuaded Joe to don a tuxedo (for the first time since their wedding). This was to be one of the most memorable evenings in her husband's life.

One by one the names of the Jaycee award winners were announced. One was a mayor of a New Jersey town and a prominent lawyer, two were engineers, the fourth was a brilliant research scientist.

"And the fifth winner," Scherer then said, "is our barber, Joe Pestana."

With this, everyone in the room rose from their chairs to

give Joe a standing ovation, the only one of the five winners to be so honored. When the applause had ended, Joe, his voice choked with emotion, could only murmur a modest, deeply sincere "Thank you."

Why should such a singular tribute be paid to a simple barber?

There are hundreds of orphan children at the Mission of the Immaculate Virgin on Staten Island, New York, who can answer this question. To them this humble and self-effacing man is "The Barber of Charity."

Joe, you see, was himself raised as an orphan. Joe was seven when his parents, because of serious economic difficulties, reluctantly had to place him, with several of his brothers and a sister, in the care of the Sisters of St. Francis at the Immaculate Virgin Mission. The orphanage, though, had to operate with very limited funds, and all too often the children had to go without the toys and other little playthings that are such an important part of childhood.

In 1943, Joe, then seventeen, left the Mission for a hitch in the Navy. As he said goodbye to his beloved teacher at the orphanage, Sister Assumpta, he said, "Perhaps some day I will be able to do something so that other orphans can have a better childhood than I had."

It was a vow Joe meant to keep. No sooner was he settled in his Navy berth than he sent a letter to Sister Assumpta, asking her if there was anything the children needed that perhaps he could get for them. His teacher replied that a radio-phonograph combination would bring many hours of delight to the Mission children.

Joe agreed that this would be an ideal gift, but he also realized that on his modest sailor's pay the purchase of such an expensive item was impossible. He tossed restlessly in his sleep that night, until a thought came to him, "Perhaps I can get others to help."

The next day he gained admittance to the office of the commander of the base, Admiral Souchek. "Could I have permission to go to the other men on the base and ask them if they would like to donate whatever they can toward the purchase of a radio-phonograph for the Mission orphans?" he asked.

"By all means," the Admiral replied. "And let me make the first donation."

Joe devoted all his off-duty time during the next two months to speaking to each of the men on the base. A shy guy usually, Joe now spoke up with great enthusiasm. "This equipment will mean so much to the orphans," he told his buddies.

When he was finally through, Joe had amassed $7,000 in donations. He sent the radio-phonograph to the Mission and with some of the money he had left over he bought a good supply of new clothing and gifts for the orphanage kids. The rest of the money would be used later by Joe to pay for some of the parties he would hold for the youngsters.

A short while after this the baker on the base told Joe that he had whipped up a huge hundred-pound cake, topped with a model of an aircraft carrier. "It's for the orphan kids," he said proudly. "It's great," Joe said, overwhelmed by the gift. "Now we've got to get it to the orphanage."

Several of Joe's other Navy buddies built a crate to hold the cake and Joe got permission to take it personally from their base at Norfolk, Virginia, all the way to the Mission on Staten Island.

"I said plenty of prayers on that plane trip," Joe now recalls. "I thought sure the cake would fall apart with every bump and jar the plane took."

As the big plane set down at Floyd Bennett Field in Brooklyn, Navy trucks speeded up and sailors helped Joe gently lift the crated cake off the plane and onto a truck, which was to take it on another jogging ride to the Mission.

Everyone at the Mission, the sisters, Joe, and the children,

Joe Pestana holds a Christmas party for orphanage children.

held their breath as the crate was opened. They all stood quietly and watched. Then they saw the "miracle." The cake was still intact. The kids smiled joyfully as the Navy cake was cut and pieces were distributed among them. It tasted just fine.

The Mission kids remained on Joe's mind and he continued to collect money and toys for them. On leaves he'd hold parties for the kids right at the orphanage.

One time Joe and several of his Navy buddies were loading a sizable accumulation of toys and gifts onto a plane that would take the "haul" to the Mission. Suddenly a little, rosy-cheeked boy came up to them. He had a police dog with him. He heard about the great need of the less fortunate boys and girls at the Mission. "I want to give my dog to the orphans," the boy said happily. "I've had so much fun with him and now I want the orphans to also have fun with him."

"That was probably the best gift we ever received," Joe now says. "That little boy gave us the thing he valued the most, his own pet."

It was at one of his parties for the orphans, this one at Christmas time, 1950, that Joe met a brown-eyed girl named Ann Sole. Ann was also trying to brighten the lives of the Mission kids. She and several of her girl friends had gotten together and were giving their own parties at the orphanage. They began to talk about their works of charity and Joe asked her for a date.

Most of Joe's Navy pay was going to the Mission. So when he took Ann out for the first time he had only ten dollars in his pocket. As luck would have it, it was also a mighty cold winter's day. But Joe wanted to make this first date a happy one for the pretty young girl who had already captured his heart.

They went to New York's Broadway area and took in a movie, sharing a good dinner afterwards. Joe's ten dollars was going fast.

It was now early in the evening. Joe only had sixty cents

left and Ann lived in Red Bank, New Jersey. He finally had to tell her of his predicament.

"Perhaps we can borrow Father Kenny's car," Ann said sympathetically. Father James Kenny was a priest at the orphanage who had been there when Joe was a boy and had been a good friend to the youngster.

Joe's last sixty cents paid for the subway and ferry ride to the orphanage.

An hour after they arrived at the Mission, Joe and Ann were seated in Father Kenny's second-hand station wagon, on their way, they hoped, to Red Bank. But a heavy snow was now falling, and the roads were almost impassable. They were right smack in the middle of a big snowstorm and, for good measure, the car itself suddenly stalled.

Along about 12:30 A.M., after Joe had worked frantically for almost an hour to get the station wagon moving again, the travel-weary couple reached Red Bank.

Their first date was over, and quite a date it was. Such an experience might well have dampened the ardor of a less enraptured couple, but as for Joe and Ann—well, they were married two months later.

When Joe had to ship out some seven months afterwards, Ann went to live in Red Bank. Their first child, Joe, Jr., was born in 1951.

Joe was discharged from the Navy in 1953 and he soon began to learn the barbering business. His family started to grow; a daughter, Juanilde, was born next, and eventually there would be six Pestana children.

Joe went to work for Ann's father, who was also a barber, and the family moved into a comfortable, fairly large apartment directly over the barber shop. Joe made sure that his family's needs were always taken care of, but he did not forget the continuing needs of the Mission orphans. He set aside just about all the tips he earned at the barber shop to buy more toys and gifts for the youngsters.

One afternoon Joe was in the shop. A heavy-set, middle-aged man was in the chair having his hair cut. The man was a Texan, in town to visit relatives. A friend of Joe's was also in the shop, and as he worked on his customer Joe talked to his friend about the new batch of toys he had just accumulated for the Mission. When the haircut was over, the man rose from the chair, drew out his wallet, and handed Joe some money for the haircut, and a couple of dollars extra. "I'm a stranger in town, but—well, here's some money for the orphans."

This is typical of the way it has gone. Friends, relatives, and perfect strangers have come up to Joe and donated what they could for the Mission kids. Joe never brags about it, but to date he has collected over $23,000 and given it all to the Mission.

For a while Joe was also deeply involved in the Cub Scout activity in his town, and here too he combined help for Red Bank's children with his love for the Mission kids. He did this by bringing busloads of his Cub Scouts right to the Mission. "I wanted to show the Cub Scouts that orphan kids are really no different from them," Joe explains. "And I also wanted to show the orphans that the Scouts visiting them were just like them. I think it helped the children to understand each other better."

For several years Joe also arranged to have the children taken out of the orphanage for short periods of time and placed in the homes of friends and interested parties to give the youngsters a feeling of being part of a real family, if only for a brief time. Joe began by taking five or six orphans into his own home and treating them exactly the same as his own children. Then his friend George Trad, a successful businessman now retired, took ten children into his home. Soon some twenty Red Bank friends and neighbors were welcoming the orphans into their families. "With the help of these generous people we were able to give one hundred and fifty orphans a chance to experience family life," Joe says. One woman who took in an orphan child for just a few days grew so attached to the youngster that she received permission to keep the child with her for a week longer.

The Pestana brood had been growing at such a fast rate that it soon became obvious that they now needed their own home. So a short while ago the Pestana family moved into an old, but still very comfortable, thirteen-room house in nearby Atlantic Highlands, which they had luckily been able to buy at a reasonable price. And Joe opened his own barber shop five blocks away.

Joe never sought any special recognition or glory for any of his charitable works. Up until a few months ago he didn't even keep a scrapbook of the stories that have appeared in the local newspapers each time Joe received an award or commendation from a civic or religious group. "I never dreamed I'd receive any awards for what I've been doing. All I want to do is help the orphanage more."

Such modesty is part of the nature of the man. As the New Jersey Jaycees expressed it when they named Joe Pestana one of the outstanding men of his state, "He has instilled joy into the hearts of thousands of children and adults."

## IV

# Troubadours of Mary

IT WAS EARLY evening. About fifty cloistered nuns stood along a grillwork fence inside the Visitation Convent in Riverdale, New York. The nuns were laughing exuberantly. On the other side of the grill was a large room. Using the floor of the outside room as an improvised stage, a small woman with a round, joyful, pixielike face was performing a rollicking comedy-monologue. The woman was Mary-Eunice Spagnola and this was the first time such a performance had taken place in this convent.

Mary-Eunice completed the first part of her performance, then left to change her costume. In the interim her husband, Joe, a stocky, gentle-faced man, came onto the "stage" and addressed his raptly attentive audience.

"Your laughter pleases us very much, for it shows us that you have enjoyed our program," the man said softly. "Perhaps you would like to know a little about us. We call ourselves Mary Productions and our performances are part of our devotion to the Blessed Mother. In our own way we are trying to do something positive to improve the field of communication. We have dedicated our work to the Message of Mary so that others may laugh, learn, and be uplifted spiritually."

Then Mary-Eunice returned to the stage, this time to deliver a serious religious monologue. Her audience listened in hushed and reverent silence, deeply moved by the presentation.

Joe and Mary-Eunice Spagnola are a married couple of just average means, yet they are freely giving of their time and energy in this unusual and inspiring personal mission in the service of Our Lady.

Mary-Eunice has been stage-struck since she was seven, back in her native city, Rochester, New York. She started by acting in school plays. Later she managed to obtain some small parts on local radio programs.

Through friends, she learned about the Rochester Blackfriars, a professional, Catholic-sponsored theatrical group in her area, which was presenting worthwhile, religiously-oriented plays. Mary-Eunice was not then a Catholic; nevertheless, she felt that she wanted to be part of such an exemplary group as the Blackfriars. She was readily accepted by them and the experience not only gave her valuable training as an actress, but it also served to kindle in the young girl an understanding and appreciation of the Church itself. She was taken under the wing of a kindly Catholic teacher, Gertrude Furlong, who recognized her God-given talent and helped her to develop and mature as an actress. The influence of her beloved teacher and of her work with the Blackfriars culminated in Mary-Eunice's conversion to Catholicism.

Soon afterwards she journeyed to New York and enrolled for intensive study at the Irving Dramatic School. She also obtained a part in a play and it was at one of the rehearsals that she met Joe. Joe, a writer and distributor for several magazines, also loved the theater. "You have so much fine ability as an actress and comedienne," Joe said to her after they had known each other for a short time. "Your talent can bring so much happiness to others. Never give up your theatrical work." His encouragement spurred the young actress on.

In April, 1942, Joe went into the Army and was sent to the South Pacific. But he and Mary-Eunice didn't allow separation to dim their romance. They simply continued their courtship by mail. Joe came home in 1945 and a year later he and Mary-Eunice were married. It was then that the young couple first vowed that they would devote all the time they could to, as Joe put it, "helping to make a better world." "We decided," he explained, "that in the field of communications we could do much to propagate worthwhile ideas. Stage plays, the press, radio, records, films, and tape recordings reach millions of people and have an important influence on our youth. Here, we realized, was a great potential for good."

The newlyweds rented a small attic apartment in Brooklyn, and Mary-Eunice, in addition to continuing her acting, began to write plays. All her plays, in one way or another, depicted the couple's devotion to Our Lady. One, for example, might be a comedy built around a typical morning in the lives of several career girls or about teen-agers at a summer camp. Or the play might be a more serious effort, telling the story of the life of St. Vincent de Paul or the life of Mother Celine, the foundress of the Sisters of the Resurrection. But whatever the subject, Mary-Eunice tried to combine in each of her plays some wholesome humor, a little education, and a little inspiration.

A year later the Spagnolas had a son, Joe, Jr. ("Jeams"). Mary-Eunice now had her hands full caring for a new baby and also continuing to write her plays. But she managed both handily.

In July, 1950, she and Joe visited their good friend Father Francis Doino, S.J., then pastor of the Nativity Church on New York's Lower East Side. They outlined to him an idea that they were very eager to express.

"We want to make our plays available royalty-free to anyone

Mary-Eunice and Joe Spagnola.

Mary-Eunice, son Jeams, and Hildegarde, who has worked with the Spagnolas.

who desires to present them," Joe said. "We're not seeking monetary gain or personal glory from the plays. All we want to do is help spread Marian truth and goodness in the field of communication."

"This is a truly worthwhile mission you both desire to undertake," Father Doino replied. "Why don't you present some of your plays in our auditorium and we'll invite people from the local parishes and religious organizations to see them. In this way we will be bringing the plays to people's attention."

This was the birth of "Mary Productions." For the next three years Mary-Eunice wrote, produced, directed, and acted in the productions at the Nativity Church while Joe held down a regular job and also served as a backstage worker, stage manager, and moral support for the venture. They built up a troupe of about fifty experienced actors and actresses who, in addition to performing at the church, also traveled throughout New York and New Jersey on "one-night stands" at churches, schools, and hospitals, wherever they could find anything to serve as a stage and a big or small audience that wanted to see them.

In 1954 the Spagnolas rented a home in Dumont, New Jersey, a move that opened new horizons for Mary Productions. Joe took a job as a taxi driver so he could have enough time for the productions. On a borrowed mimeograph machine, hundreds of copies of Mary-Eunice's plays were run off and Joe began to distribute them to little theater groups throughout New Jersey, and even in other states.

In the spring of 1957, the Spagnolas were in their car riding along a smooth country road in New Jersey, looking for a good but moderately priced house that they could buy. Joe took a wrong turn and they found themselves in the small town of Belford. "That wrong turn proved to be a right turn for us," Mary-Eunice recalls. "We were immediately enchanted by this quiet, rustic town and the friendly faces of the people we saw walking, not hurrying, along the town's pleasant, tree-shaded streets. Then we saw it—a little gray, seven-room house at Number 58 Lenison Avenue. On the porch was a 'For Sale' sign. That's the house, I said to Joe, and he quickly agreed."

A few days later the little gray house became the home of the Spagnolas and the "For Sale" sign on the porch was replaced by a small sign that read simply MARY PRODUCTIONS.

When her son began to attend school, Mary-Eunice was able to devote more time to her playwriting. With Joe, she also started to conduct speech and drama classes for grammar-school children in her area. This provided them with enough of a livelihood so they could also continue their apostolate in the field of communications.

Mary-Eunice wrote over a hundred plays and monologues. Mary Productions was becoming well known. Hundreds of requests for the scripts poured into the Spagnola home each month. They were coming now from all over the world. It was a tremendous job, but Joe filled every request.

A group of girls in Altoona, Pennsylvania, travels about performing Mary-Eunice's plays in churches and hospitals. Especially at Christmas and Easter, the festive seasons, a Legion of Mary group performs the plays at homes for the blind and homes for the aged as well as at hospitals for people with serious illnesses.

Students at St. Mary's School for the Deaf in Buffalo, New York, perform the plays for audiences of other deaf students, who follow the play's action and dialogue by lip reading and through watching the pantomine of the actors.

Missionaries in Africa, India, and South America are also using the plays, with native students as their actors, to teach God's word to their flocks. A short while ago one of Mary-Eunice's comedies was presented by missionaries before an audience composed entirely of aborigine children, inhabitants of Palm Island off North Queensland, Australia. These children had always been shy and retiring, but the play brought them completely out of their shells. They sang and mimicked right along with the actors. The play had brought the youngsters closer to the Church.

The plays have had an effect for good not only on the audiences, but also on the actors themselves. One young girl played a nun in a production of Mary-Eunice's stirring anti-Communist play, *Message of the Century*. Later the girl herself became a nun. "Although this girl had always been deeply interested in the religious life," Joe says, "we like to think that perhaps appearing in that play helped her to finally decide that she could best serve Our Lady by seeking a religious vocation."

The Catholic Daughters of St. Mary's in New Monmouth, New Jersey, set out one afternoon for the town of Wayne to perform Mary-Eunice's play *Hope of the Morrow*. They had chartered a bus for the long trip. The company's wardrobe, props, and other heavy equipment meant an added burden for the bus driver. "This is a bigger job than I thought it would be," he said, with definite annoyance in his voice.

When the troupe arrived at their destination, there was the big job of unloading all the equipment and lugging it into the large theater where the performance was to be held that night. The driver helped, but he wasn't too happy about the extra work.

"Why don't you come in and watch the play?" one of the members of the troupe asked him when they had finished unloading the bus.

"Well, I guess I might as well," the driver said matter-of-factly. He took a seat in the back of the auditorium. The play unfolded and with its development a strange change took place in the driver's feelings. The beauty and inspiration of the play itself and the sincere, heartfelt performances of the hard-working actors moved the man deeply.

After the performance the man went to work again helping to lug all the equipment back to the bus, but this time he worked without complaint. Now it was not a job, but a privilege to be part of this very worthwhile activity.

"You people are wonderful," he said with a smile of contentment. "Call on me anytime. I'll be glad to help you." The troupe had found a friend for life.

To date, over ten thousand copies of Mary-Eunice's plays have been distributed in more than forty countries and six continents. The scripts have been translated into many languages, including Japanese, Chinese, Spanish, and French.

Off the northeast coast of Australia lies the remote and primitive island of Fantome. Here the Franciscan Missionaries of Mary maintain a leper colony. Joe had visited the colony in 1943 while in the service and had then voiced the hope to the missionaries that perhaps some day he could do something to help the lepers. Today that hope has been realized. The lepers now have their own theatrical group, thanks to the scripts Joe is providing for them. "It is very satisfying for us to know that God's afflicted ones are now gaining some comfort and joy from our efforts," Joe says.

In the summer, with their classes closed, the Spagnolas pile into their car, the back of which is filled with costumes, make-up kits, props, and spotlights. For the Spagnolas are now going on tour to entertain audiences personally with sketches and monologues. Jeams, who is now a handsome eighteen-year-old, has been made a "junior co-partner" in the troupe. He travels with his parents and takes roles in the productions. Their tour takes the family to the heart of big cities as well as to tiny, out-of-the-way hamlets. One night they'll be performing at a little church in New York City's Chinatown before an enthusiastic audience of Chinese and Italian residents of the area. On another night they'll be playing in the Caugnawaga Indian village, nestled by the great Saint Lawrence Seaway near Montreal, Canada. Here they presented Mary-Eunice's monologues on the life of Tekakwitha, the Indian maiden who was converted to Catholicism and who many hope will one day achieve sainthood. Dressed in her colorful and authentic Indian costume, Mary-Eunice looked so much the part that tourists stopping at the village asked her to pose for snapshots so they could show the folks back home "what a real Indian looks like"!

Their summer travels will take the Spagnolas up into Canada and along the eastern seaboard of the United States. And always, no matter where they are asked to perform, they will ask only that people donate within their means toward their expenses. The only gain they seek for themselves is the satisfaction they feel in bringing the message of Our Lady and wholesome entertainment to thousands of people.

In December, 1960, Frank Hamilton, the program director for Radio Station WFHA-FM, located in Red Bank, New Jersey, heard about the good works of the Spagnolas and asked them if perhaps he could help bring their message to more people. "I'll be pleased to let you broadcast from my station," Hamilton said.

"This is a golden opportunity for Mary Productions," Joe replied in gratefully accepting Hamilton's offer.

The Spagnolas now conduct four 15-minute programs beamed every Sunday morning over Station WRLB-FM in Long Branch, New Jersey. One relates stories about Our Lady and her devotees; another is aimed especially at the blind, the handicapped, and shut-ins and consists of inspirational verses, short stories, and brief talks. The third program comprises interviews with people that are helping better their own communities or any part of the world, especially in the fields of communication, education, and charity. The fourth is composed of songs of the Faith.

Tapes of the programs are being circulated, just like the plays, to all parts of the world. Missionaries, like the La Salette Fathers in Quezon City in the Philippines, are playing the tapes on their own radio programs, thus beaming the voices of Joe and Mary-Eunice and their message of Mary to the native multitudes.

Mary Productions continues to expand. Joe and Mary-Eunice are looking now toward their entry into television and motion pictures so they can reach many more thousands. "Good people decry the lack of worthwhile purpose of much that exists today in the field of communication," Joe points out, "but Mary-Eunice and I feel that criticizing the bad things being done isn't enough. We believe that everyone should make whatever contribution they can toward improving the field of communication so that it can become, as it has the potential to become, one of the greatest influences for good that man has ever known."

# V

## Jerry Walsh Walks Again

THE DOCTOR LOOKED gravely at eighteen-year-old Jerry Walsh as he told him the bad news. "I'm afraid you have rheumatoid arthritis. It's very serious. You will probably be confined to your bed for the rest of your life. At best we can hope you may be able to get around in a wheelchair."

The diagnosis struck the gangling, dark-haired Irish lad very hard. Here he was, a star athlete, a guy who could run about with great vigor and win baseball and football games almost singlehandedly, and now this physical strength and athletic prowess of which he was so boastful was gone.

That was more than twenty-five years ago. Today Jerry Walsh, now in his early forties, is very far from being bedridden or even from having to use a wheelchair to get about. As special educational consultant to the Arthritis and Rheumatism Foundation, Jerry travels thousands of miles each year, all on his own. No, he hasn't been cured of arthritis. His legs are still stiff from the hips down and he has a crippled left hand, but by using just one crutch and a cane he has completely overcome his affliction and is just as active and mobile as the average person.

Married, with two adopted children, Jerry is now not only leading a normal life but he has also dedicated a major share of that life to helping other handicapped men and women get back on their feet just as he has done. That he has succeeded in this purposeful mission is attested to by the fact that a short while ago President Johnson named him the "Handicapped American of the Year" and cited him for "surmounting his own handicap to become a useful American citizen" and for "helping encourage, inspire and facilitate the employment of other handicapped persons."

Jerry freely admits that his own remarkable victory over his handicap was a direct result of his solid spiritual upbringing. He grew up in Columbus, Ohio. His father, a railroad brakeman, and his mother were devoted Catholics who early inculcated in Jerry, their oldest child, and his two brothers and one sister, a deeply felt love of God and a high sense of religious purpose.

As a youngster Jerry dreamed of becoming a priest. Often he would cut out a strip of white cardboard, put it around his neck, and then gaze at himself in the mirror to see how he looked in a Roman collar. He wondered, though, if he really had the special, God-given capabilities for the priesthood. "If it is God's will that you become a priest, then you will become a priest," his loving mother would say to him when he expressed these doubts to her.

Each morning he would serve at Mass in the church near their home, then head for his first class at St. Thomas Aquinas High School. After classes he could usually be found on the school's playing field, using his fast pitching arm to win for his team.

Then the family was suddenly hit by two heartbreaking tragedies. First, his brother Jimmy was drowned and a short while later his father was killed in a freak train accident while on his job.

"Those were sad days for the Walsh brood," Jerry now recalls. "But they were also the time for all of us to reaffirm our faith in God and trust in His will. It was this faith that kept all of us going. My mother went to work to support the family and my brother Frank and I also took odd jobs after school to help out."

Every spare moment he had Jerry spent engaging in the athletics he loved so much. One day while he was involved in a particularly action-packed game a scout from the Boston Red Sox baseball team came by the field to watch him. He had heard considerable talk around Columbus about the pitching prowess of this young lad, so he had come to see for himself. He watched while Jerry's pitching arm whipped the strikes across the plate and won the game for his team. Greatly impressed, the scout took Jerry aside and told him, "I think you have the makings of a Big League star. Why don't you try out as a pitcher for the Red Sox?"

It was a mighty tantalizing offer, holding forth as it did the promise of a lucrative career as a professional athlete. Jerry was then about to be graduated from high school, where he had been an honor student, and he had already made tentative plans to enroll at Providence College, a preparatory school for the Dominican Order in Providence, Rhode Island. This offer from the scout would mean a drastic change in his life plans, if he took it.

He mulled the offer over carefully for a few days and discussed it with his family. Finally he told the scout his decision. "I think I should get my college degree first," he said and the scout agreed that he had made a wise choice. In September, 1940, Jerry Walsh started his freshman year at Providence. It was also about this time that he first began to feel some stiffness in his legs but he just dismissed it as probably the result of too much ball playing.

A few months later Jerry's college days came to an abrupt

Jerry Walsh and son Jimmy.

end. His family's debts had piled up far beyond the ability of his mother to handle them on her own and still keep him in school, so he obtained a leave of absence from Providence and went to work for the Columbus Recreation Department, teaching athletics to young boys. His dream of becoming a priest was now further away than ever.

On a Saturday afternoon in June, 1941, Jerry was playing baseball on a neighborhood sandlot. The first batter from the opposing team had just taken his place at the plate. Jerry was playing in the outfield that day. Suddenly his knees began to buckle and he toppled to the ground. He was carried home on a stretcher and later the examining doctors reached agreement that it was rheumatoid arthritis.

"When they said I would probably be bedridden for the rest of my life my first reaction was one of utter disbelief," Jerry now recalls. "It just didn't seem possible to me at the time that I could no longer run around. I told my mother, 'Don't worry, I'll have this thing whipped in three months,' and at the time I was sure I would."

The three months passed and Jerry's condition grew worse instead of better. He was in constant, intense pain. The slightest movement by anybody in his room caused him excruciating agony. "As I lay there in bed, unable to move for long periods of time, I thought why me? Why should this happen to me? What had I done to deserve this? The thought came to me that perhaps God was telling me in this way that I had been too vain and boastful about my physical agility. Or perhaps He was giving me a sign that he didn't want me to become a priest, that He had something else in mind for me, something just as important and needful in its own special way as the priesthood."

The family pitched in to pay for his soaring medical expenses. His mother uncomplainingly took on a second job and his brother Frank, who was now in the Army, sent home just

President Johnson named Jerry Walsh the "Handicapped American of the Year."

Jerry Walsh, his wife Ann, and their two children.

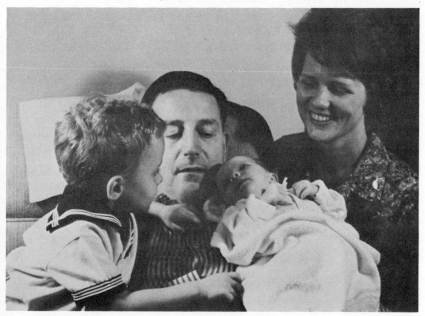

about all of his service pay each month. His sister Rosemary nursed him.

"My mother again gave all of us an inspiring display of courage in the face of this new family crisis," Jerry remembers. "Because of her encouragement I continued to say my prayers and rosary. Prayer was a very important part of my mother's life. Some years later when she learned that she had an incurable cancer she relied even more than before on the solace her prayers had always given her. She was saying her prayers as she peacefully fell into the final coma before her death."

"This was the great lesson I learned from my long ordeal with arthritis," Jerry further recalls, "that though I had lost the use of my legs, I hadn't lost what was more important than anything else, my soul. My physical strength was now gone but I was still one with God and the realization of this gave me the confidence and courage to fight on. All around me I could see that good was resulting from my suffering. Through nursing me for such a long time my sister decided to become a professional nurse. Thus my illness led her to the service of the sick and the afflicted. And during the times when I couldn't bend my knees I was comforted by the knowledge that my family and my friends were at that very moment bending their knees in prayer for my recovery, gaining more grace for themselves. I was certain that this was all part of God's design."

Despite the fact that he remained bedridden for seven and a half years, Jerry managed during this time to build up his own successful greeting card business at home. It was also during this time that he embarked on the first phase of his personal crusade to help others among God's afflicted ones.

It started with a story about him that appeared in a Columbus newspaper. Other handicapped and bedridden residents of the city read the story and contacted Jerry. They then began to keep in constant communication with each other by phone.

All of them had learned, like Jerry, to live with their afflictions and had built up successful home businesses for themselves. As Jerry explains, "We were people of different faiths and different afflictions but we had one common bond—not one of us felt sorry for himself."

It was Jerry's idea that they finally meet each other in person and talk over their mutual problems and the whole subject of the needs and wants of the handicapped. A hall in downtown Columbus was hired for the occasion, and on a warm summer night Jerry and four of his telephone friends were borne into the meeting place on ambulance stretchers.

From that modest gathering was born Courage Incorporated, now a nationally known organization with more than five hundred members. "Our purpose is to promote courage, confidence, and cooperation among the handicapped," Jerry, who was one of the organization's directors for its first ten years of existence, points out. "We inform the handicapped as to just what agencies will be able to get them jobs or, if they are confined to their homes, how they can set up their own businesses at home and thereby be self-supporting. We also made arrangements with the Ohio State University to send teachers to tutor home-based handicapped people in skills they could master despite their afflictions."

When someone with a very serious handicap would lament to Jerry, "How can I possibly support myself like this?" Jerry would reply, speaking out of his own tough but spiritually strengthening experience, "You must do the best you can with what you have. Worry about what you *can* do, not what you can't do."

Jerry's courageous example was to inspire hundreds of others. Once all-but-beaten handicapped men and women would find new determination to overcome their afflictions because of Courage Incorporated and would go on to become successful architects, painters, writers, accountants, typists, telephone salesmen, and to fit into many other useful and self-sustaining occupations.

In 1948 Jerry set out on the final leg of his journey to full physical recovery. He entered the famed Mayo Clinic in Rochester, Minnesota, where he bravely underwent two grueling operations. And each time as he was being wheeled into the operating room the doctors and nurses in attendance could hear him repeating softly to himself the prayers his mother had taught him. Several more months of exhaustive exercises and treatments followed but in the end Jerry actually walked out of the Clinic on his own two feet, helped by a crutch and a cane.

Deeply grateful to have his physical strength back, and also humbled by the immeasurable debt he knew he now owed to God and to the great doctors at Mayo for restoring his health, Jerry decided that he could best repay his debt by dedicating his life to helping and inspiring handicapped people.

He sold his successful greeting card business and resolved to spend his every working hour in the service of the afflicted. He joined the staff of the Arthritis and Rheumatism Foundation, first in Columbus and later as its field representative in the Middle West.

In 1955 Jerry, who up until then had been a "confirmed bachelor," was introduced at a parish party to a pretty, raven-haired Scottish girl, Ann Elizabeth Crawford, and the love light in their eyes soon made it apparent that Jerry's bachelor days were about over. They were married just one year after they met.

"Ann gives me patience and understanding, but never pity," Jerry says gratefully. "This is just the way it should be. No handicapped person wants to be pitied. Rather, they want to be treated as individuals with a worth and dignity of their own and to be considered just as capable, in their own way, as anyone else."

Ann's great faculty for understanding extends as well to Jerry's important work with the Arthritis and Rheumatism Foundation, though this work takes him away from her and their two small children, Jimmy and Mary, for long periods of time. In one recent year, for example, Jerry visited 161 American cities, traveling more than 123,000 miles. As Ann puts it, "Jerry speaks before religious, management, labor, and women's groups explaining to them the plight of his twelve million fellow arthritics in the United States. He tells them what individual citizens can and should do to obtain better treatment and greater understanding of arthritis sufferers and to spur increased research that will ultimately find a cure for what is now America's Number One crippler. This work is so important and needful that it is worth any sacrifice on our part to accomplish it."

Jerry also devotes considerable time to combating the countless quack arthritis "cures" that swindle desperate arthritis sufferers out of an estimated quarter of a million dollars a year. Jerry testified twice on this appalling problem before the United States Senate's Special Committee on Aging, and his testimony paved the way for the adoption of legislation to prohibit the false advertising of worthless "medical" devices and products for the cure of arthritis.

Jerry's aid to the handicapped also includes spiritual help. An active member of such Catholic organizations as the Knights of Columbus and the Holy Name Society, Jerry works through these groups to organize special retreats and special confessions for the handicapped and to make arrangements for the transporting of handicapped men and women to church services and other parish activities.

"Many people say that the Cross looks like a plus sign. Well, my cross has indeed been a plus sign for me," Jerry affirms resolutely. "I've lived a fuller, more meaningful life because of having been felled by arthritis in my youth than I would probably have lived otherwise. I've been able to help more people than if I had become a baseball player, or even perhaps a priest. I'm sure this was the way God wanted it."

# VI

# Young Drug Addicts
# Are His Friends

THE TEEN-AGE GIRL, her small, pretty face pale and tense, walked hurriedly through the hospital corridor until she saw a volunteer worker. "Is Dad here? Can I speak to him?" she asked in an anxious voice. The girl was a patient at Riverside Hospital, a special institution open at that time in New York City for the treatment and rehabilitation of adolescent drug users.

The volunteer worker knew immediately who it was the girl wished to see. "I'll get him," he said.

The girl slumped onto a bench-seat near the corridor and stared blankly ahead as she waited. A few minutes went by; then the person she so anxiously wanted to see came up to her. He was a tall, white-haired man, with a gentle smile brightening his face.

"Dad, can I speak to you for a little while?" the girl asked pleadingly.

"Of course, for as long as you wish," the man replied softly, as he settled himself beside her.

As they spoke, the girl started to relax. Calmly, and without hesitation, she related the step-by-step process that had brought

51

her to the terrible agony of drug addiction. The man listened attentively and the girl knew that he sincerely understood her problem and would not condemn her for her failing.

"Several of the other patients here at Riverside told me I could speak to you frankly, that you are a kind man, and now I know that they are right," the girl said as she reached the end of her story.

"It is good that you have told me all this," the man said. "You have sinned, but now you realize how wrong you were to start using drugs."

"Yes, I do," the girl replied with great feeling.

"Remember that despite your failings God loves you. Let us go to Communion together so you can begin your new life."

The girl rose from the bench, a smile of deep contentment now on her lips. For the first time since she had entered the hospital, the teen-ager felt that she had the moral strength necessary to overcome her fearful addiction.

The man who had produced this remarkable change in this young girl is Thomas J. Egan. To the teen-age drug addicts he has befriended, he is known simply and affectionately as "Dad." At a robust eighty years of age, Tom Egan is conducting his own apostolate to teen-age drug users. By teaching them the catechism and by showing them kindness and understanding, Tom has helped hundreds of young victims of drug addiction become, in Tom's words, "physically and spiritually whole again."

Tom Egan's own youth was spent amidst the green fields and good people of the small county of Offaly in Ireland. Tom's father was a hardworking farmer who cared as best he could for Tom and his twelve brothers and sisters.

"Though we had modest means, we were a happy, tightly knit family," Tom recalls. "There was mutual trust and respect in the Egan household, rooted as it was in the religious beliefs of my mother and father who instilled those beliefs in all of us, thus fortifying us against evil influences."

Thomas ("Dad") Egan (fourth from left), his late wife, and the Egan family.

In 1907, when hard times came to his beloved Ireland, Tom, then seventeen years old, had to leave home and make his way to America.

He settled in a crowded section of New York and held down some odd jobs for a while. Then he learned of the opportunities available on the New York City police force. Here, he decided, was the place for him to find security and also to do something constructive for the community. Starting as a simple patrolman, Tom quickly rose through the ranks. His own solid upbringing made him especially adept at handling young boys and girls who had gotten in trouble with the law. "I realized," he said, "that what many of these youngsters needed, more than punishment, to straighten themselves out was the same kind of sympathy and understanding that my parents had given me when I was a boy. These youngsters had been denied this proper parental guidance. They were the products of broken homes and bad environment, which had molded their character in the wrong direction."

It was Tom's job to transfer the young boys and girls from the juvenile courts to correctional institutions. At first the youngsters looked upon Tom with the same resentment and belligerence they felt toward all policemen. But Tom soon won their friendship. He listened to their problems and offered them whatever help he could. All told, several hundred youngsters were put in Tom's charge, and only one ever tried to escape from his custody. "That one was immediately brought back by several of the other youngsters, who told her she should be ashamed of giving me trouble," Tom recalls with considerable pride.

One evening at a church meeting Tom was introduced to an attractive, dark-haired girl named Mary Beirne. She immediately captured the handsome Irish lad's heart. They were married on April 23, 1913, and their first child was a son, whom they named Tom. The Egans were to have seven sons and two daughters. (One daughter would die in infancy.)

As a member of St. Benedict's Church in the Bronx, Tom became the parish's first lay chairman of their annual Catholic Charities drive. A devoted and tireless worker in all drives, Tom built up a long list of solid accomplishments for the church and became a mainstay of St. Benedict's First Saturday devotions.

In 1952, with an unblemished forty-year record to his credit, Tom retired from the police force, leaving with the rank of lieutenant. But for a man with Tom's unaging energy, retirement meant only the chance to devote more time to helping and counseling young people in trouble.

Tom became custodian of the House of the Good Shepherd, in Peekskill, New York. The House, which is a haven for wayward young girls, is maintained by the Sisters of the Good Shepherd. It was a major part of Tom's job to transfer the young girls from Girls' Term Court in New York to the home, a trip of some forty miles. Many of these young girls had had their adolescence scarred by bad experiences and were now bitter and hard to get along with. But Tom's warmth and sincerity easily won their confidence and respect.

One 17-year-old girl that Tom brought to the home was a drug addict. But Tom could see that she was intelligent and sensitive, and that she had just gotten into bad company. "I was sure she wanted to be set on the right path," Tom says.

Tom visited her every day at the home. They spoke together like father and daughter, and Tom told her about the Catholic faith. Although the girl was not herself a Catholic she began to become interested in the church. Tom told her all about Catholicism and how it could give her life new meaning.

One day, as Tom once again came to visit her, the girl suddenly exclaimed, "Please, Dad, will you pray for me to become a Catholic?"

"Of course," Tom replied. A short while later Tom's prayer

was answered when the girl told him she was embracing Catholicism.

A few weeks afterward the girl had another request to make of Tom. "Please, Dad, will you pray for me to become a nun?" Tom again said that he would be happy to pray for her, and then he added, "On the day you receive your habit, I hope you will invite me to be there."

The day did come, and it was a proud and thrilling one for Tom, as he watched the young girl he had counseled take her sacred vows. Today the girl is a sister at an upstate New York convent. Tom still hears from her from time to time, and in a recent letter she told him joyfully, "I am happy now to be at the foot of the Cross."

Tom was custodian at the home for about three years, and during this time his kind and gentle ways helped to ignite the spark of faith in many a previously "mixed-up" youngster and return them to the grace of God.

Late in 1956 Tom's dear wife, Mary, was suddenly taken seriously ill and Tom had to give up his work at the home to care for her. The Egan children were now full-grown. Five of the boys were married and two other sons, Daniel and Alcuin, were now Graymoor Friars. Tom and Mary lived in a comfortable white frame house on a quiet street in the Bronx, a house that Tom had built himself. Once a year the entire Egan family would gather inside the house, Tom and Mary's seven sons, their daughter Veronica, and their twenty-three grandchildren.

When Mary's health started to improve, Tom asked his daughter if she would like to accompany him on a European vacation that would take them to several countries, but especially to Ireland, for it had been exactly fifty years since Tom left the treasured scenes of his childhood.

"It's going to be a wonderful trip," Tom exclaimed excitedly as he and his daughter began to make their plans for the journey. But shortly before they were scheduled to leave, Mary again was taken ill and on January 23, 1957, Tom's beloved wife died.

It was a sad time for Tom, being without dear Mary after forty years of a richly blessed marriage. But Tom's faith in God's will remained strong. "Veronica decided to go ahead with our plans for the trip," he recalls. "We knew that Mom would have wanted us to continue and that she'd be with us in spirit."

Early in May, 1958, Tom set foot again on the soil of his fondly remembered Ireland. The townspeople of his village gave him a rousing welcome, making his all too brief stay a memorable occasion.

On his return home Tom again plunged himself into church activities. One day his daughter told him about the work being done at Riverside Hospital by a number of Legion of Mary members. The Legion members, including housewives, nurses, and professional and business workers, were volunteer workers at the hospital who accompanied the young patients to Mass on Sundays, assisted them through the Dialogue Mass, and talked with the youngsters afterwards, trying to help them with their problems, both material and spiritual. They also called back to the Sacraments those youngsters who had been away from them for some years.

Riverside Hospital, Tom knew, was established in July, 1952, by the city of New York exclusively for the treatment and rehabilitation of teen-age drug users who voluntarily committed themselves to the institution. A devoted and competent medical staff worked hand in hand with volunteer helpers from such groups as the Legion of Mary to help restore these troubled teen-agers to wholesome lives.

Through his work in the New York police department, Tom was well aware of the terrible and growing problem of narcotic addiction among teen-agers. He had seen the shocking statistics revealing that 72 per cent of drug addicts under thirty years of age had first been "hooked" on narcotics when only adolescents. And he had also seen beyond the statistics to the young people themselves, who could be leading useful, constructive lives, but who through foolhardiness and lack of proper guidance were now doomed to the "living death" of drug addiction.

Tom's own New York City has become the focal point for the distribution of illicit narcotic drugs throughout much of the United States, and it was here that the problem of teen-age addicts was especially acute. It has been estimated that in New York City there are some 4,000 narcotic addicts under twenty-one years of age and at least 4,000 more teen-agers on the verge of addiction.

"I was thinking, Dad," Tom's daughter said right after she told him about the Legion of Mary's work at Riverside Hospital, "you've always been able to get along so well with young people, to win their confidence and friendship, and in this way help them. Perhaps you can become a volunteer worker at Riverside."

Tom reflected deeply over his daughter's suggestion. The need was indeed great, he realized. Still, he was now seventy-four years old and had retired to a pleasant, easy life. Should he now start such strenuous work?

Several days went by and Tom was still mulling over his daughter's idea. Then he read again in a newspaper about a group of teen-agers who had been arrested by the police in a narcotics raid. It was then that Tom reached a fateful decision. "I must help them if I can," he said to himself with firm determination.

The officials at the hospital were startled and a bit surprised at first when Tom came to them and said he would like to be a volunteer helper at the institution. Should a man of Tom's age undertake such physically taxing labor? they wondered. At the

the same time they admired his spunk and determination; finally they gave him permission to work with complete freedom at the hospital.

On an August morning in 1959 Tom Egan arrived for the first time in front of the entrance of the hospital and looked up at the imposingly tall gray-brick buildings sprawled across a good part of North Brothers Island, set in the middle of New York's East River. "I was a little nervous that first day," Tom now recalls. "I couldn't yet know the difficulties that I would encounter in this work, but I was sure there would be obstacles that my faith would have to overcome."

The very first teen-age patient that Tom befriended seemed to be reacting favorably to his good counsel. She realized how wrong she had been to start using drugs and, with Tom's guidance, she was building within herself the moral strength that would keep her from plunging back into the darkness of addiction when she left the hospital. But shortly after leaving she again succumbed to the terrible temptation of drugs and had to return to the hospital.

"There were several failures like this in the first few months of my work at Riverside," Tom now remembers. "Still, I believed that I could reach at least some of the unfortunate teen-agers. This kept me going in the face of my early setbacks."

One morning a sweet-faced, sad-eyed, 17-year-old girl stopped him in one of the hospital's corridors.

"I have heard from some of the other patients here what a kind man you are," she said sincerely, "could you instruct me in your faith?"

"Of course," Tom replied, and he began to teach the girl the catechism. The girl became a Catholic and when it came time for her to leave the hospital, she said to Tom, "I had thought it would be too difficult for me to become a Catholic, but you have shown me that it isn't difficult at all if one really wants to be part of the Church."

Tom assisted the girl in finding a new home in an upstate New York community so that she could begin a new life away from the bad environment that had exerted an evil influence over her before.

Fired by his first success at the hospital, Tom went ahead with renewed dedication, seeking out other young patients at the hospital whom he thought he could help and who genuinely wanted his assistance. One teen-age girl that he took under his wing had been but a year away from graduation from college when she had fallen in with bad company and was arrested in a narcotics raid.

Through Tom's persuasive and kindly counsel, the girl became a convert to Catholicism. When she left the hospital, she told Tom pridefully, "I feel as though I have been reborn." A short time later the girl was married. "I was godfather to that fine young couple's first child," Tom says with a proud smile.

Another time a teen-age boy sought Tom out at the hospital. The boy was deeply troubled. He had started using drugs when he was only fourteen years of age. To pay for his very expensive habit he had become a "pusher," working to get other teen-agers "hooked" on drugs.

"You realize the terrible damage you have done to yourself and to other young people," Tom said firmly, but with a tone of forgiveness and understanding in his voice.

"Yes, what else can I do besides repent?" the boy asked tearfully.

"Now you must have courage," said Tom. "You must tell the priest all you have told me."

The boy went to confession and to Communion, and when he later left the hospital, Tom was sure he was a completely changed young man. "I recently received a letter from him," Tom says. "He's married now and living on the West Coast. He has a good job and is living a decent, respectable life."

"All this boy needed," says Tom with conviction, "and all

most of these troubled young people need to set them right, is charity and kindness. I treat them as human beings. I recognize that they are victims of circumstance who have foolishly turned to drugs as an escape from their bad upbringing and evil environment. If people would sincerely offer them help these youngsters could be saved."

Tom has found that often the parents can also help. One mother had completely disowned her teen-age daughter when she learned that the girl had become a drug addict. Tom immediately phoned the mother. "If your daughter is to be helped," he told her, "she must know that her mother loves her and wants to help her fight her terrible addiction. Won't you try to understand your daughter's problem and try to help her?"

A few days later the girl rushed up to Tom and with a bright and happy smile on her face exclaimed, "I just received a letter from my mother! Isn't that wonderful, Dad?"

When the girl left the hospital she was accompanied by her mother, and Tom is confident that this girl is now on the road to recovery.

Tom spent three days a week at the hospital. Each Wednesday he would also first drive to St. Joseph's Seminary in Yonkers, New York, to pick up two seminarians who would go with him to the hospital and help him with the religious instruction of the young patients he was helping. This meant about six hours traveling time, but as this hearty Irishman puts it, "I didn't mind it at all."

Tom also kept track of his young friends when they left the hospital. He directed each one to a parish in their neighborhood and encouraged them to take an active role in church activities. By offering this personal "after-care" to his teen-age charges, Tom helped them get back on their feet and also kept them from falling back into the clutches of the evil dope pushers who had first tempted them to try narcotics.

Any misgivings that the hospital's officials may have had when Tom first proposed that he work with their young patients completely disappeared. Tom commanded the respect and admiration of the hospital's entire medical staff, as well as that of the other volunteer workers and the hospital's chaplains of all faiths. Moreover, Tom received a special medal from the hospital in recognition of his outstanding achievements at the institution, the only nonprofessional man to be so honored.

Father M. Archangel Sica, O.F.M., who was the Catholic chaplain at Riverside until the closing of the hospital a short while ago, observes: "Tom's success with young drug addicts is the direct result of the good example he sets for the youngsters. He is the living proof to them that there *are* good people in the world who are sincerely concerned about their welfare. By going to Communion *with* his young friends he shows them how his own personal devotion to the Faith has given him a good life, and that they too can find happiness and contentment if they but get their souls in order and with him come closer to the Blessed Mother."

All of the other volunteer workers at the hospital were considerably younger than Tom and, as one of them said, expressing the feelings of the others, "Tom could just as well be sitting at home taking it easy, living out his senior years without a care. But being concerned only for himself isn't part of the nature of this truly remarkable man. Tom would never be content to ignore any youngsters in trouble when there's a chance he can help them."

The closing of Riverside has not curtailed in any way Tom Egan's personal mission to young drug addicts. He now works with these troubled youngsters in several New York City hospitals. As Tom says, with a deep smile of pride and fulfillment, "My life is blessed."

# VII

# Dolores Hart: From Stardom to the Convent

WHERE IS Dolores Hart today? You probably remember this radiant and delicate young actress for her deeply moving portrayal of St. Clare in the film *Francis of Assisi*, or as the victim of Nazi barbarity who finds a new faith in the goodness of people in the film *Lisa*, or in about a dozen other important motion pictures.

Of late, however, you have probably noticed that this gifted and natural young actress has been missing from our movie screens. There's a good reason for this. A short while ago, within the quiet serenity of the Regina Laudis Monastery of the Benedictine Sisters in the tiny Connecticut farm village of Bethlehem, Dolores Hart became Sister Judith.

Dolores turned her back on a glamorous and luxurious Hollywood career because of her deeply felt conviction that only in a religious vocation would she find true happiness and contentment.

Msgr. Arthur F. Terlecke, who was her pastor in Chicago for many years, explains Dolores' faith-inspired decision in these words: "It was something she has always wanted. Her best picture was *Francis of Assisi* because in private life she was

63

so much like a nun. As an actress she remained a daily communicant and made two or three retreats each year."

Nor was this a hasty decision on her part. Rather, her choice of the religious life was the culmination of her own lifelong search for spiritual fulfillment.

Born Dolores Marie Hicks, she had a difficult childhood. Her parents were divorced when she was four, and she lived with a succession of relatives after that. When she was ten she was put in the care of her grandparents, who lived on the Northside of Chicago. She was not then a Catholic, and until then her only real contact with Catholicism had been through a grand aunt, for whom she was named, and who was a nun in a convent in Georgia. The grand aunt would sometimes visit Dolores' parents when Dolores was just a small child and she always remembered her aunt's speaking of the peace and serenity she had found by embracing the Catholic faith. "I'm sure my grand aunt was praying for me," Dolores would say later.

Her grandparents sent her to St. Gregory's School, only because this was the closest school to their home and they feared ten-year-old Dolores might be injured if she had to walk too far to school each day.

This simple act of concern for their young grandchild proved to be providential. Dolores attended Mass each day with the other children at St. Gregory's. Dolores would later recall this time and say, "I was deeply impressed by the wonderful sense of belonging that the children derived from their practice of the religion. And as I participated with them I also began to have this same feeling of belonging. I had been exposed to other churches of other religions as a child, but it was only here that this sense of joyousness and purpose came over me. I now felt that I was home, that here was where God was."

The precocious youngster decided she wanted to be a Catholic. "It was a conscious, willing decision on my part,"

Dolores Hart

Dolores was convinced. "Some people are quick to say that any child who had no more roots than I would clutch at anything with a solid foundation. That doesn't bother me, they're only admitting that the Church has strength and stability."

To her happy surprise, her grandparents offered no opposition to her conversion. "The greatest moment of joy in my life was my Baptism at the age of ten," Dolores would later say without hesitation. At eleven she was confirmed.

Eight years later she was enrolled at Mary Mount College in Los Angeles. At a school dance she met a very sincere and serious young man named Don Barbeau, who was attending nearby Loyola University. Don had been a Trappist monk, but reluctantly left because of poor health. He was immediately attracted by Dolores' qualities of naturalness and honesty. "Have you ever thought of being an actress?" Don asked. Dolores quickly shrugged off the idea. Though her father had been an actor and she had done a little acting in school plays, an actual career as an actress was the farthest thing from her mind. But Don persisted. "We're putting on a production of *Joan of Lorraine* at Loyola. You'd be perfect as St. Joan. Come down and try out for the part," he urged her.

Dolores couldn't say no to such enthusiasm. She read for the part and landed it. Then Don told her, "I'm going to send your photograph and some information about you to Hal Wallis at Paramount studios and ask him to come down and see you as Joan."

Wallis never did come to a performance of the play and Dolores decided that this one production would probably be the extent of her acting career.

One afternoon a short while later, Dolores was seated in a classroom at Mary Mount, intently listening to her teacher explain the day's lesson. Suddenly one of her girl friends burst into the room, shouting, "Dolores, Dolores, Paramount Pictures is calling!"

Dolores Hart as St. Clare in the 20th Century-Fox film
*Francis of Assisi.*

It was Hal Wallis' office. Though he wasn't able to see her in the play, he had been greatly impressed by Don's letter and by the photo of her. "Would you come in for an interview?" Wallis' representative asked.

The rest, as they say, is movie history. Dolores passed her screen test with flying colors and was given a seven-year contract by Wallis. At Wallis' urging she changed her name from Hicks to Hart.

The movie-going public took an immediate liking to the wholesomely attractive young girl and she was quickly featured in one hit film after another, appearing with such long-established stars as Montgomery Clift, Anna Magnani and Anthony Quinn. And she scored another triumph with her critically-acclaimed role in the long-running Broadway play, *The Pleasure of His Company*.

Dolores made up her mind that her sudden fame wasn't going to turn her head. "I knew that this gift of grace had been given to me with a condition, that I try not to set up any false principles and try not to let the glitter and make-believe trappings of Hollywood delude me into forgetting the grace I had been given."

Dolores began speaking before Catholic and interfaith groups, especially youth groups. "I tried to convey to others my own conviction that everyone needs God and that faith can be a great buttress against one's own shortcomings and weaknesses, helping us to rise above them and give our lives true purpose," Dolores said.

In 1960 she received the exciting news that she had been chosen to play the part of St. Clare in the large-scale 20th Century-Fox film, *Francis of Assisi*. "I was both overjoyed and frightened by the challenge of this great part," Dolores told me. "Here I was to play this very vital and courageous woman who was about my own age and whose life, like mine, involved an inspired conversion. In her case, of course, it was a conversion that caused her to turn her back completely on the material luxuries of the world and follow St. Francis. To me, playing St. Clare would be a work of love, and I undertook the part with all my heart."

Before the actual filming of the movie began, Dolores made her own journey to Assisi. For five and a half weeks she hiked across the beautiful Italian countryside, where the atmosphere of the Middle Ages is still faithfully preserved. She walked along the same byroads and paths St. Francis himself used and she stood in awe-inspired silence at the very places where St. Francis had worshipped. Of especial importance to her was her visit to the shrine in the crypt at Santa Chiara where the remains of St. Clare are now on public view. "Before I had come here, I had always thought of saints as being something not quite real. But as I now looked at the remains of this very devoted woman, I realized that she, and indeed all saints, were human beings first, who then became saints through their superior love of God."

Dolores' role in the film *Lisa* was a challenge of a different kind. In this film she played a Jewish girl who had suffered unspeakable treatment in a Nazi concentration camp. Upon her release from the camp the girl feared that nobody cared for her any more because of what had been done to her. But through a renewal of her faith in herself and in people she was able to return to a normal life.

When she was first asked to play the role, Dolores wondered if she, a devoted Catholic, could find any identity with this young girl who believed in a different faith and thereby make the character believable on the screen. "I spoke to a friend of mine, who had also been in a concentration camp. Like all the others who had survived this terrible experience, my friend asked herself why she had been chosen to suffer this inhumanity. But she came to realize that by returning hate for hate she would be no better than the people who had put her in the camp. This, I realized, was part of my own faith. But it was by recalling my own childhood that I finally found identity with the young girl in the film. I remembered that I had also thought people didn't care about me, but in the love of God and the love of the people that I discovered in the Catholic faith I realized someone did care for me, and I brought this same feeling of love to the role of the girl in the film."

A short while after she made *Lisa*, Dolores came to her decision to, as St. Clare had done, turn her back on worldly riches and instead commit herself fully to a religious vocation. Asked why she decided to do this, Dolores could only reply with heartfelt simplicity, "A vocation is hard to explain. Those who have it need no explanation. None is possible for those who don't."

But probably we can find the real reason why Dolores Hart is now Sister Judith in the words of a good friend of hers who, after visiting her at the Monastery, said, "There is such beautiful serenity in her face. She has truly found her fulfillment in life."

# VIII

# Neighbors Get Together

It is an early evening in a quiet, tree-shaded street in the Long Island suburban community of Uniondale. A man in shirt sleeves approaches the door of a handsome, stucco-type house. Held carefully under his arm is a large metal box. He rings the bell and in a few seconds he is welcomed at the door by the man of the house. They exchange friendly greetings. Then the visitor relinquishes the metal box to the man and after a warm handshake departs.

On that same evening, this rather strange-looking ritual is also taking place at some nine other homes in and near this community. In fact, it takes place *every* night at ten different homes in this vicinity.

What's going on? It's all very simple, and at the same time deeply inspiring. The metal boxes, you see, each contain a statue of Our Lady of the Rosary and a large string of beads —a rosary. They are being passed from family to family as part of this community's own, unique method for encouraging more widespread family rosary devotion. To date, more than thirty thousand Rosaries have been said in this deeply earnest "chain of faith."

71

The first link in the chain was forged in 1961 on a day in October—the month of Our Lady of Fátima. It was a pleasant afternoon and the members of the Holy Name Society at St. Martha's parish in Uniondale were on their way home from a religious retreat. Two of them, Tom Leavy and Lou Garavente, were seated in the back of the bus discussing a matter of some urgency. A few days earlier Tom had been asked by his Catholic Action co-chairman to deliver a talk on the import of Our Lady's message at Fátima at the next Holy Name meeting, and Tom was concerned about how he could make his talk more meaningful.

"Talks of this kind usually wind up as purely academic speeches, and after they're over nobody really does anything to help spread Our Lady's message in a more direct and significant way," Tom observed thoughtfully.

"I've been thinking much the same thing," Lou remarked. "I heard that at St. Martha's school the children take turns bringing home for one night a statue of Our Lady. This greatly encourages them to say the Rosary. It seems to me that there's the germ of an even bigger and more all-embracing program in that idea if we can develop it."

The two men mulled over the idea for several days until they had developed a plan, which they set down on paper. At the next Holy Name meeting, after Tom had delivered his Fátima talk, Lou rose from his chair and advanced their plan to the other members. "It's certainly worth a try," everyone agreed, and thus Uniondale's unique Rosary Crusade was born.

First, a committee of seven members of the Society was designated to draw up a letter explaining the idea. The letter was sent to each family in the parish. It didn't take long for the responses to arrive. Some seventy families wrote saying they wanted to participate.

The founding families were divided into four groups, with

Blessing the Crusade's first statue and rosary on the
Feast of the Immaculate Conception, 1961: Andrew
Palumbo, Catholic Action chairman; Father Dennis
O'Brien; moderator of St. Martha's Holy Name Society;
John Guarino, Holy Name president; and Tom Leavy,
Catholic Action co-chairman.

Clem Schuerlein leads his family in the recitation of the Rosary.

*Thomas F. Moloney*

from fifteen to twenty in each group, assigned according to the closeness of their homes to one another. Each group was to select a captain, who would start the chain by saying the Rosary first in his own home with himself and his family gathered before the statue that belonged to his group and using the beads that were to travel with it. Then, before seven thirty the next night (so that the younger children in the family could also participate) he was to deliver the statue and rosary in their metal box to the next family, who on the next night, before seven thirty, would take it to the next family, and so on. This meant that each family would receive the box again about every two or three weeks. In addition, all the families would be encouraged to make a nightly recitation of the Rosary together, even when they didn't have the statue and beads in their possession.

The carrying on of the Rosary Crusade had an almost immediate effect for good in the community. Clem Schuerlein, father of thirteen, recalls, "We had tried a number of times before the Crusade to have regular family Rosaries in our home, but it never seemed to work out. Something usually came up at the last minute to distract us. But now, receiving the statue and beads in this way, we are constantly reminded of what Our Lady told us at Fátima, that the Lord desired devotion to her Immaculate Heart to be established in the world. That if this was done, many souls would be saved and there would be peace. She also asked that Russia be consecrated to her Immaculate Heart, that the faithful make a Communion of reparation on the first Saturday of each month, and that we should say the Rosary, and say it properly. The deep sincerity prompting those leading the Crusade to start the program inspired us to make a greater effort to emulate their loyalty. The family Rosary is now very much a regular part of our family life."

The Crusade served the added good purpose of helping to

restore the father to his rightful place as the head of his family. As Lou Garavente, the present chairman of the Crusade, puts it, "In all too many homes today the father faces difficulties in commanding the respect he should receive. This can be especially true in suburban communities, where the father is away at work much of the day, and what with commuting time and all, doesn't see as much of his children as he should and therefore often loses touch with them. But now, seeing the father leading the family in the Rosary recitation, the children gain new respect for him. My youngsters and the other children in the Crusade families now look forward with great anticipation to the day when their turn comes for the statue and the beads."

As word of the project spread throughout the community, more links were added to the chain of faith as more families joined to make up new groups. More than two hundred families now take part in the Rosary Crusade.

Early in 1962 the Crusade leaders decided that it might be a good idea for all the families to get together at least once a year for a mass public display of their devotion to Our Lady. Mother's Day was chosen for this occasion for, as Tom Leavy explains, "We all felt that since this was the day on which we honored our earthly mothers, it would also be the most appropriate day to pay tribute as well to our Heavenly Mother."

On that Mother's Day in 1962, a bright sun washed over the crowd of some five hundred who gathered in the courtyard of St. Martha's school for the Crusade's first outdoor Fátima Devotion. A great outpouring of religious fervor filled the air as Father Denis O'Brien, the moderator of St. Martha's Holy Name Society, led the assembled parishioners in prayer.

Gratified by the community-wide acceptance of the outdoor devotion, the Holy Namers decided to add an indoor devotion to the Crusade program. They chose October, in honor of Our Lady, for this second religious event.

Early on the afternoon of October 28, the members of the Crusade families, with the exception of the fathers, gathered inside St. Martha's Church. As the ceremonies began, the men marched into the church carrying lighted candles and reciting the Litany of Our Lady. Walking in front of them was a small group carrying a statue of our Blessed Mother. The procession halted in front of the altar, where the statue was set down. Then the men, as a body, began the recitation of the Rosary, answered by the other members of their families.

On Mother's Day, 1963, a second outdoor devotion was scheduled, but this time it looked as though the Crusade might run into a serious problem. As Kiernan McCarthy, a Crusade captain, recalls, "The sky was heavy with rain clouds that morning and it looked like we'd have to call the whole thing off, sad as this would be. But I prayed to my own patron saint, Saint Jude, and you know, at noon the sun came out strong and clear and we had an overflow audience of more than six hundred. Now more than ever we were convinced that God was blessing our efforts and the Mother's Day and October devotions are now regular yearly events in our community."

Has the Crusade achieved its original purpose of helping spread the Fátima message in a more meaningful way? Father O'Brien believes that it has. He considers the Crusade idea "one of the most effective methods yet devised for encouraging families to say the Rosary together. In addition, the Crusade shows how much good laymen can do by working together on their own in this way for their Church and community."

One family in the parish had suffered a tragic loss when their teen-age son was killed in an accident. The tragedy embittered the family and they fell away from the Church. Then a neighbor told them about the Crusade. Here, they saw, were other families, many of them also touched by personal tragedies and problems, now gaining the strength to face life's hardships through the faith and devotion that united them in the

Rosary Crusade. The family asked to join, and the night the statue and beads were brought to their door was the night the family was reborn in the faith.

In another home in the community, the father had become complacent in the practice of his faith. He refused to attend church and his wife and children had to attend by themselves. Then the family joined the Crusade and through it the father underwent an amazing transformation. Seeing the dedication of the other families and the great sense of personal joy felt by the other fathers as they led their families in the nightly Rosary recitations made this father realize how he had failed both himself and his family by failing his religion. And one Sunday morning, a short time later, after a twelve-year absence, he was again sitting with his family in their pew at St. Martha's.

Another family in the Crusade was also struck by tragedy one summer's day when the father died suddenly. Two and a half nights later the statue and the Rosary came to the door of the stricken home. More than before, the family needed the comfort and courage that the Rosary recitations had always given them. Thus, that night the remaining members of the family carried out their Rosary devotion just as before, then passed on the statue and beads to the next family in their group.

The Crusade families are proud of the fact that their chain of faith has never been broken. It continues all year long, every day, without interruption. And the Holy Name Society that started it all is expressing its devotion to Our Lady in other ways as well. Every meeting of the Society opens with the recitation of the Rosary, and the Society itself has been consecrated to Our Lady. In addition, the Society holds an essay contest each year for the students of St. Martha's parochial school, awarding statues of Our Lady to the writers of the best essays on "What the Rosary Means to Me."

As Tom Leavy affirms, "The prayers of one family are but

one small candle, but now, with the advent of the Crusade, we have the glow of the candles of many families throughout our community, and in time in other communities as the idea spreads, and this will make a great and powerful illumination to be sent heavenward to bring to all the world, we prayfully hope, the blessings of lasting peace and brotherly love."

## IX

# *Dedicated Dramatist*

THE TITLES FLASHED on the television screen announcing that afternoon's presentation of "The Catholic Hour," an original play by Robert J. Crean entitled *Once There Was a Postman*. A close-up of a man seated before a typewriter loomed up over the final title, then the thoughts of the man, later identified as a writer, were heard. "I was born and raised in a town named Indian Orchard—a remarkable name for an unremarkable New England town," said the voice. "Not a glamorous place. There were mills along the river where the French and the Irish and the Polish worked. And although most of them were Catholics, when they went to church on Sundays they went to the "Irish" church or the "French" church or the "Polish" church. Up on the hill were white houses and a New England square and the one and only Protestant church. A mill town in Massachusetts where the divisions between people were clear-cut and peacefully maintained. I didn't know it then, but there was one man who broke through those lines. The postman. He was welcomed in the tenements down by the river and up on the hill where we lived. He was my father."

Few in the TV audience watching this program were aware

79

that they were seeing more than just an engrossing and thoughtful play on the relationship between a father and his son. Bob Crean, the play's author, had actually dramatized an important aspect of his own life, right down to using the actual names of the places and people of his youth. In this way he was paying his respects to his late father, who had first imparted to him the dedication to high ideals that is now the motivating force in his successful writing career.

The lanky, bearded, thirty-nine-year-old playwright, father of eight children ranging in age from a year and a half to ten, is a shining example of how a Catholic can help raise the spiritual level of our popular arts. Bob's plays have been presented on just about all the leading television dramatic programs and he has been the recipient of numerous awards, but the acclaim and financial rewards that his success has brought him have not diminished in any way his devotion to his ideals. "I've turned down writing assignments when I felt that they wanted me to write something that could have a harmful effect on others and that would be incompatible with my own belief," Bob says with deep sincerity.

Bob's father died peacefully, his rosary held gently in his hand to the end. Bob remembers vividly how just about everyone in the town of Indian Orchard came to the funeral parlor, including the Mayor, the town bankers, the young and old, the rich and the poor. "My father was loved by everyone who ever came in contact with him," Bob recalls, "and looking back on his life I realize that this was because he gave so much of himself both to his family and to everyone. It was because of his good example and influence that I first thought of becoming a writer."

In addition to being a postman, Bob's father also worked as a part-time newspaper reporter. Often at night he would be seated before his battered typewriter, pounding out a story, with Bob looking on over his shoulder. And when Bob himself began to write he started on that same typewriter.

Robert J. Crean

"My father encouraged me in my writing ambitions," Bob relates. "He taught me to disregard the risks and to be what I wanted to be." Bob's writing debut was, as is often the case, fairly inauspicious. He was attending high school in Springfield, Massachusettes, at the time, and heard that the famous singer Jeannette MacDonald was stopping off briefly in town. The young boy talked his way into an interview with her and then hopefully dispatched his article to the editor of the Springfield *Daily News*. The paper not only published the interview but the editor also gave Bob his first by-line.

After graduating from high school Bob continued to pursue his writing aspirations. He landed a job with the Springfield *Morning Union* as a proofreader and was soon given a chance as a reporter.

With the outbreak of World War II Bob, then nineteen, enlisted in the Army Air Force and was eventually assigned to Westover Field near Springfield as a gun-sight specialist. One afternoon a buddy of his suggested that they make a weekend retreat at the Passionist Monastery near the camp. That retreat proved to be the next great influence in Bob's life. "The strong sense of personal dedication of the Passionists really inspired me," Bob says. "Frankly, up until then I was just a 'Sunday' Catholic but when I came away from that retreat I knew that my creative insights as a writer would be greatly enriched in the sacraments, in prayer, and by the insights of Catholicism."

A short time after his discharge from the service early in 1947, Bob was reading a Catholic magazine and his attention was caught by an article relating the story of Reverend Gilbert Harke's much-praised drama department at Catholic University in Washington, D.C. That very night Bob's application for admission to the college was in the mails, and a few days later he received word that he had been accepted.

Lecturing at the university on playwriting was Walter Kerr,

drama critic of the New York *Herald Tribune* and noted Catholic layman. "Kerr proved to be the next important influence in my life," Bob states. "He showed me that a writer can present universal truths without writing shallow propaganda for the Church. I realized that it isn't necessary to have a priest or a nun in a play for that play to reflect the insights of our religion. Rather, this can be done if the play gives people a vision of the world as God made it. As Kerr pointed out, people are searching for order and a play should show them a vision of this order. From this new image of man that the writer shows them, people gain in both mind and soul."

Bob had several of his first playwriting efforts performed at the college. In one of them his leading lady was a young graduate student in the drama department named Katy Simonaitis. Dark-haired and pert, Katy loved to laugh, but she also had her serious side, and she and Bob were immediately drawn together by their mutual interest in the arts. They dated steadily for about two years until Bob received his B.A. and Katy her M.A. in drama at the University. On May 31, 1951, they were married.

The newlyweds settled in Washington, D.C., and Bob went to work for the NCWC News Service and the *Catholic Standard* as a reporter and drama critic. Their first child, Cathy, was born on March 31, 1952.

Two years later the Creans made a fateful decision. They would move to New York City, where Bob would have more opportunity to try his playwriting wings. While holding down a full-time job as an advertising copywriter for a New York textbook company to support his family, Bob continued to work at night and on weekends on his plays.

His first big break was not too long in coming. While working for the NCWC Bob had interviewed many celebrities, among them the popular comedian Peter Lind Hayes. Hayes had taken an immediate liking to the sincere young man, and when he learned that Bob was now living in New York he offered him a job as one of his staff writers. This marked Bob's entry into the then very young field of television. When Hayes read some of Bob's plays he was greatly impressed by their power and importance and he brought them to the attention of his agent. Through them, Bob sold his first play to television, a one-hour drama, *Anna Santonello,* a sensitive and moving portrait of the problems of living of an Italian-American family.

The drama was shown on the Kraft Theater program on an August night in 1956. The next day *Variety,* the show business chronicle, called Bob "an exciting addition to the ranks of top-flight TV dramatists." More of his scripts were soon sold. In fact, he became the only playwright to have three hour-long shows on television in the same month.

Bob also made another good friend, Dick Walsh, the dynamic young producer of "The Catholic Hour" TV program, who asked him if he would do some plays for him. Although the financial rewards were quite a bit lower here than for commercial television fare, Bob eagerly began to turn out scripts for Walsh. As Bob explains, "I like the program because it gives writers complete freedom to express their ideas. Nothing has ever been changed in my scripts for 'The Catholic Hour.' The show is a real joy for writers."

Unfortunately, this freedom with responsibility did not apply as well to commercial television. More and more of Bob's regular scripts were being drastically changed for the worse, without his permission. Once the completely unnecessary element of divorce was pushed into one of his scripts at the insistence of the show's leading lady. Another time a bishop in Bob's script was changed to a governor because the show's producer feared the bishop character would offend non-Catholic viewers. (Bob was so angered by these arbitrary changes that he insisted that his name not appear on the credits of the show.)

Finally Bob had had enough. Despite the temptations of fame and big money that commercial television offered, Bob decided that he had to be true to his beliefs above any other consideration. He quit writing for commercial television entirely. While still turning out scripts for "The Catholic Hour" and other religious-oriented programs, Bob also turned his attention to an area in which he knew he would have complete artistic and spiritual freedom—the stage.

Bob spent about a year working on his first stage effort, a play about American Catholicism and how it affected the lives of several people. (The play, entitled *A Time to Laugh,* opened in London a short while ago and is slated for a Broadway production in the near future.)

It was not until late in 1960 that Bob decided to return to commercial television. "I found that in the interim the medium had grown up quite a bit in its treatment of serious writing," Bob explains. "Television producers were now looking for new and interesting dramatic subjects, and they had suddenly discovered that religion can be interesting and provocative."

One writing assignment that Bob was especially pleased to carry out was an hour-long script for the Armstrong Circle Theatre on the martyrdom of Bishop James E. Walsh, the courageous and unyielding Maryknoller imprisoned, and still held incommunicado, by the Red Chinese on trumped-up spy charges. It was an assignment that was not without considerable challenge for the young writer. As Bob pointed out to this writer, "I wondered if I could really do justice to this saintly, intelligent, and erudite man. Since Bishop Walsh is still in prison I couldn't interview him. How, then, could I successfully capture his true character and spirit?"

Bob decided that he could perhaps solve his problem by thoroughly studying the Bishop's life. He therefore set out for Maryknoll, New York, where he was welcomed and encouraged by the Maryknoll Fathers. At Maryknoll, he read everything that was available on Bishop Walsh and everything that the valiant churchman himself had written. From some of Walsh's létters Bob was able to extract lines of dialogue that would fit into his play and that would faithfully re-create the manner in which Walsh would speak to his friends, to his parishioners, and to his Communist tormentors. "A definite personality slowly emerged from my research, the personality of a rare and real person, and this was the way I conceived him in my script."

Bob's play, as presented on television, drew high praise from the TV critics. The Maryknollers themselves, many of whom had known Bishop Walsh personally, complimented Bob on the authenticity of his script. The play itself is now being shown in many parochial schools.

Bob is equally proud of the four-part series he did for "The Catholic Hour" on *Prejudice—U.S.A.* The presentation examined prejudice against Catholics, Negroes, and Jews as seen through the eyes of a typical Catholic family. Bob pulled no punches in exposing the religious and racial tensions of our society. His series showed not only prejudice against Catholics but also the deep-seated prejudices harbored by some Catholics themselves against other religious and racial groups.

"We of course received many letters of praise for this series, but we also received a number of letters from Catholics criticizing us because we had shown prejudiced Catholics," Bob recalls. "These letters were as welcome as those that praised us because they showed me that I had accomplished what I had set out to do: to rouse Catholics as well as non-Catholics out of their complacency about prejudice, and to stir Catholics to a re-examination of their own personal behavior in the light of the clear anti-prejudice teachings of the Church." The series earned for Bob the Bronze Brotherhood Award of the National Conference of Christians and Jews and brought a total of five important awards to the producers of the program.

In April, 1959, the Crean brood settled in a ramshackle,

ten-room house in Larchmont, New York, overlooking Long Island Sound. The place was a hundred years old and in serious need of repair, but Bob, Katy, and their older children went to work putting it into livable shape.

Bob's workroom is tucked away on one side of the house and the family knows that when he's in it he's not to be disturbed, except *possibly* in case of fire. Bob starts his creative labors at about nine each morning, and keeps going with little letup until about three thirty. This is when the older Crean children stampede into the house from their classes at the nearby Ursuline School and the house gets a little too noisy for further writing. Bob then goes over his mail and attends to his letters and phone calls. He spends the balance of the day with the family, either down at the ocean beach near their home or walking with some of his youngsters along the quiet, tree-lined streets of the town.

Bob's time with the children ends early in the evening when he says the Family Rosary with each of them, including his babies, then settles them into their beds.

On many an evening Bob will be addressing some nearby religious or civic group (he especially likes to talk before youth groups) on why he feels Catholics should have more awareness of the arts. Bob feels strongly that "there is a need for Catholics to be brave and go into the arts, instead of just emphasizing the dangers there. This is the only way we can influence for good our mediums of mass communications."

His own writing apostolate reached one of its high points in 1958 when his five-part "Catholic Hour" series, *Family—U.S.A.*, received first prize at the Catholic Television Festival in Monte Carlo. It was a moment that Bob's father would indeed have been proud to witness.

# X

# How Bill Gargan Licked Cancer

"I'm sorry to have to tell you that you have cancer of the larynx," the doctor quietly said.

The man seated before him, who received this terrible news, was veteran motion-picture and stage actor William Gargan. It was a November afternoon in 1960.

The red-haired, rugged, 55-year-old performer had been appearing in the national company of the play *The Best Man* when he developed a lingering sore throat. "Nothing to worry about," he thought at first. "I've just been using my voice too much."

The show had completed its run in San Francisco and was scheduled to open next in Chicago when it was discovered that no theater in the Windy City was available at that moment.

Bill Gargan is convinced that this turn of events was actually, in his own words, "one of those mysterious ways in which God works. Because we had no theater in Chicago we had to close the show prematurely. So I returned to my home in Beverly Hills and decided to see my doctor about that persistent sore throat."

And so Bill—and Mary, his wife for thirty-four years—learned the worst. It was cancer.

"What can be done?" Bill asked the doctor.

"We'll have to operate to remove your larynx. It'll mean that you won't be able to speak again in your normal voice."

A long pause followed. As an actor, Bill depended on his voice for his livelihood. What would the future hold for him without a voice?

"Do I have any choice in the matter?" he asked.

"There are just two choices," replied the doctor. "Operate and live, or don't operate and die."

Bill reached for Mary's hand and held it tightly. He drew a deep breath. "When do you want to operate?"

"I'd say in about two weeks."

The Irish grin returned. "It will take only about two days for me to get all my affairs in order. Can you operate then?"

The doctor studied the actor's face. "Okay. I'll try to clear the decks so we can operate in about two days."

The next two days were a time of deep reflection for Bill Gargan.

A long-time member of the Church of the Good Shepherd in Beverly Hills, he was drawn to spend a good part of his waiting time within the church in thoughtful prayer.

"As I sat there, I said to myself, Why me? Why my voice? But as I continued to pray, another thought came to me. Perhaps God had an important reason for all this. Perhaps now there was something else He wanted me to do with my life, something that required that I first lose my voice. I wondered what that reason was."

On the evening of November 9, Bill, with Mary walking alongside, was wheeled to the operating room. As they neared the door Bill chose the last words he would ever speak in his natural voice. "I love you, Mary," he said.

Three and a half hours later the operation was over and

Bill was conscious, resting comfortably in his bed. The doctors gave him the good news that they believed they had caught the cancer in time. Although a period of five years must pass before it can be said with certainty that a cancer will not return, the doctors assured Bill that chances of a recurrence of the malignancy were remote.

Then Bill's doctor pulled a chair close to the bed and told the actor about a remarkable new method by which people who had had their larynx ("voice box") removed could actually speak again.

"It works like this," the doctor explained. "You will be taught to take air into your mouth and swallow or force the air into your esophagus by locking your tongue to the roof of your mouth. When the air is forced back up, it will cause the walls of the esophagus and pharynx to vibrate. This action will vibrate the column of air in the passages and you will be able to produce a low-pitched sound. Then, by using your tongue, lips, teeth, and palate just as normal people do, you will be able to articulate this sound into words."

Bill's ruddy face brightened with a smile.

"I must tell you," added the doctor quickly, "that it won't be easy. Learning this technique will mean a great deal of hard work."

The patient scribbled something on the pad in front of him and handed it to the doctor. It said simply, "When do we start?"

Bill Gargan's never-say-die response to this new challenge was no surprise to anyone who knew him well and understood the circumstances of his background.

Reared in a tough, crime-ridden section of Brooklyn, Bill learned before he was ten that it was the kid with courage to spare and a don't-back-down attitude who had the best chance for survival.

His mother was a schoolteacher. His father earned a modest

Bill Gargan and Gregory Peck, Crusade Chairman of the California Division of the American Cancer Society.

living as a contractor. Between them, they managed to keep young William and his brother Eddie on "the straight and narrow."

Both parents cherished a secret hope that Bill might enter the priesthood. But during his years at St. Francis Xavier grammar school it became apparent that the big, good-looking Irish lad's interests lay in two other fields—amateur theatricals and athletics. Proof of one was the scream of joy that exploded from the boy on the day he received an elocution medal at school for excellence in his class play.

Bill attended St. James High School. After his graduation he went on to college. But the necessity to help his parents with the support of their home soon forced him to leave school and go to work.

In his first important job he was a private detective. But Bill—who some years later would play television's tough-talking private eye, Martin Kane—failed to make the grade as a real-life "gumshoe." There followed for Bill a succession of odd jobs, including work as a salesman, payroll guard, bill collector. This last employment proved to be the most ill-fitting of them all. Bill was too good-natured. He loved people too much to kick them when they were down.

Once he was sent to the home of a destitute family to collect a long overdue bill. The woman sobbed out her sad plight to him: her husband was out of work and she was desperately struggling to take care of her family. Since Bill also had experienced poverty and privation, his immediate impulse was to sympathize with the family. He left the house without collecting the money. To cover himself with his boss, he wrote the word "deceased" across the face of the bill and resolved never to tell the impoverished family what he had done.

A short while later, the woman came to the collection agency's office, very much alive. Her husband had found a job and she was there with the money to pay the bill. When

Bill Gargan speaks to a group of laryngectomees, who
six weeks earlier successfully completed their lessons in
the new method of speech.

Gargan's boss learned what had happened, that was the end of Bill's career as a bill collector.

Bill's brother Eddie, who also liked acting, had managed to snare a part in one of the big hit plays of the 1920's, *Rose Marie*. While attending a theatrical party with Eddie, Bill was introduced to LeRoy Clements, a noted producer who had just co-authored an upcoming Broadway opus called *Aloma of the South Seas*. Clements took one look at the second Gargan—handsome, broad-shouldered Bill—and immediately demanded, "How would you like to be an actor? I've got a part for you in *Aloma*." Bill accepted gladly.

His professional acting debut was in the bit part of a Tahitian coconut-picker. By the time *Aloma* completed its long run on Broadway, Bill Gargan had appeared in every male role.

There followed several years of tough trouping for him. He appeared in a few more Broadway plays, some of them flops. When there was no work on Broadway, he accepted any roles he could land in stock and touring companies.

In 1928 he took a long enough vacation to marry his childhood sweetheart, Mary Kenney. Their marriage would eventually be blessed with two sons, William, Jr., and Leslie and, to date, two grandchildren.

Bill's ingratiating performance as the prizefighter-turned-butler in the hit comedy of 1932, *Animal Kingdom,* won him the New York Drama Critics Award for that year and skyrocketed him to the top of his profession.

Hollywood called. Bill appeared in some 110 motion pictures, among which the most memorable were *Cheers for Miss Bishop*, *The Bells of St. Mary's* and *They Knew What They Wanted* (for which he received an Academy Award nomination in 1939).

Bill came back to New York in 1948 with an idea for a new television series in which he would star. The program would be built around the exploits of a tough and daring private detective, Martin Kane. The show was produced and enjoyed a successful two-year run with Bill in the lead.

In 1955, he went to Europe to film thirty-nine half-hour TV segments based on the same character. This popular series is probably still playing on some television screen somewhere in the world.

Challenges met and challenges overcome shaped Bill Gargan's life before his cancer operation, and the pattern was not to change afterward.

With the help of his wife and under the guidance of the American Cancer Society, Bill started the painstaking exercises required in order to learn a whole new way of speaking. For half an hour a day over a sixteen-week period, Bill kept at the lessons. Many times he would falter, frustrated and exhausted, but Mary encouraged him to start again and persevere despite the difficulties.

Four months later, his training in the new technique just about over, Bill spoke his first words. Though his new speaking voice was hoarse and had something of the quality of an echo, the words did come out clear and audible.

From then on, the actor was on his way to eventual mastery of the technique. "The more I used the method the better I became, until I was able to speak with complete ease," Bill says pridefully.

With this new lease on life, Bill plunged back into his work. He appeared as a mute clown on a television dramatic show and—as befits an old trouper—came through this first professional challenge after his operation without a flaw. Encouraged by this success, he decided to become a producer and director. Soon he was flooded with job assignments.

But Bill's conscience was not at ease. As he explains it: "I felt that God must have pulled me through that operation successfully and let me hang around longer for some really important purpose, beyond just the start of my professional life again.

"Then it came to me that perhaps I had been put through this ordeal of losing my normal voice so that I could be in a position to help other afflicted people in some way."

Bill therefore asked the American Cancer Society if they could suggest some way he could help promote their good work.

A society official told him, "Why don't you speak to other people like yourself who have lost their normal speaking voices —other laryngectomees—and show them how you've licked this handicap? You can be an inspiration to many people."

It didn't take more than a few minutes for Bill to decide to accept this proposal and to undertake this enormous new job.

From that moment, his time and energy were almost totally invested in his new "calling." He traveled over 40,000 miles as a volunteer worker for the Cancer Society. He raised funds for the crusade to find a cure for cancer. He visited scores of hospital wards and clinics, always seeking out other laryngectomees.

"I had the same experience as you," he would say to them, adding, "Let me tell you about this wonderful method by which you can learn to speak again. . . ."

One such visit was to the National Hospital for Speech Disorders in New York City, where he spoke before a group of some thirty laryngectomees.

"Sure I felt depressed when I first realized that I would never speak again in my normal voice," Bill told them. "But now I'm here to tell you that you have nothing to fear. You can learn to speak again!"

He told them one of his favorite stories, the one about the well-dressed man carrying a violin. Lost in Greenwich Village, he spotted a beatnik and asked how he could get to Carnegie Hall. The beatnik drawled: "Practice, man, practice."

"That's the secret," Bill urged the patients. "Apply yourself to the training program until you've got it. Never give up."

Some weeks later, Bill returned to the hospital, this time to congratulate those same thirty people. They had successfully completed their lessons in the new speaking method. Now they all voiced their personal debt of gratitude to the man whose example had inspired them to keep at it.

Recently, the Catholic Actors Guild honored Bill Gargan with an award in recognition of "his contribution as a participant in or patron of the performing arts and whose further contribution to the American scene has been of outstanding significance."

Bill accepted the award modestly, saying that he considered it a privilege and a responsibility for him to help in the rehabilitation of others.

"I've been entertaining people for over thirty-five years. But as much as I've loved acting I've never had a greater feeling of satisfaction and personal joy than I've gotten through this work."

He grinned. "I guess that's why I'm still around."

# XI

# "Mom" Levy and Saint Joseph

MANY RELIGIOUS ARTICLES and figures adorn the comfortable, tastefully furnished, thirteen-room Levy home in New Rochelle, New York. But one has special significance. It is a small figure of St. Theresa, and it has been set in a prominent place near the front door. Wilfred Levy, a truck driver for the New York State Department of Public Works, had found this statue lying on the ground, along his regular route. Its base was broken, which was probably the reason why it had been discarded. But Wilfred decided that, damaged or not, the statue should still have a home, and this both Will and his wife, Celestine, have handsomely provided.

"Will and I just feel that nothing and no one should be homeless," Celestine explains simply.

Inspired by this deeply felt concern of theirs for the homeless and the abandoned, the Levys, a middle-aged Negro couple of just average means, have, over the years, opened their hearts and their home to scores of foster children, orphans, foreign and American college students in need of a temporary place to live while they continued their studies, and many others, both young and old, who needed their help.

Celestine Levy knew at first hand the sadness of being brought up away from one's family. Her mother was a Negro, her father white. Her parents separated when she was nine years old and her mother had to work hard to make ends meet.

Although, Celestine's mother was not then Catholic, she decided, nevertheless, to enroll her child in the Catholic school near their home in New Rochelle. She did so because Catholics had always been kind to her. She recalled that when she was a child living in Virginia the Catholic church in her home town was the only one that allowed whites and Negroes to attend services together in the same building, although the law required that they had to sit in separate sections.

At the Church school young Celestine was first made aware of the Catholic faith. The religion deeply impressed the young girl and it wasn't long before she was asking her mother if she could become a Catholic. Her mother raised no objection and indeed a few years later she too would wholeheartedly embrace the Faith.

The year was 1917 and at the time there was no welfare agency that Celestine's mother could turn to for assistance in lightening her great burden of having to work full-time and also care properly for her child. She therefore reluctantly decided to place Celestine in a home. She chose St. Benedict's Home for Destitute Colored Children in Rye, New York. (The law at the time required that Negro and white children had to live in separate homes.)

"But it was not so bad for me as for some of the other children at the home who had no families at all," Celestine recalls. "My mother would visit me at least once a week, while the real orphan children at the home received no visitors at all. But my mother was a very kind and generous woman and after visiting with me she would also visit with as many of the orphans as she could. She became a family for them."

Set in a clearing near the home, and surrounded by a grove

of graceful walnut trees, was a majestic garden in the center of which was an imposing statue of Saint Joseph. The children from the Home would often come to this lovely spot to pray, and it was here, one summer's day in 1920, that young Celestine offered a very special prayer. It was a prayer for the children at the home who had no families of their own. "I promised Saint Joseph and Our Lord that in later years, if I was able to, I would find a real home for these orphans," Celestine recalls. Such was the heartfelt beginning of her devoted crusade for the homeless and the abandoned.

Celestine left St. Benedict's at the age of sixteen and went to live with an aunt while she completed her high school studies. One day, a few years later, a girl friend introduced her to a handsome young man named Wilfred Levy. (Will had acquired his last name from his grandfather, a West Indian Jew. Many of Will's relatives still live on the island of Jamaica.) Celestine had her first unchaperoned date with Will and soon they were dating steadily.

The happy occasion of their marriage, in 1926, was followed by deep sadness when Celestine lost her first three babies by miscarriage, but God blessed the Levys in November of 1928 when their only child was born, a daughter, who also was named Celestine.

The Levy family moved into a small, cozy apartment on West 97th Street in New York City in an interracial neighborhood. One day two Sisters from the Helpers of the Holy Soul mission in their neighborhood came to their door. They were taking a census of the Catholics in the parish, and Celestine asked them if there was anything she could do to help ease at least part of their heavy work load. "We have been trying to arrange catechism classes for the Catholic children of the neighborhood who attend public schools, but we have been unable to find a suitable place near their homes that wouldn't overly tax our small financial resources," they told her.

Celestine Levy plays the organ at a "family" gathering.
Mrs. Levy beams on Debbie Barrios, daughter of her
first foster child.

"Why don't you hold the classes right here in our apartment?" Celestine eagerly suggested.

For some time thereafter, on three afternoons a week, the Levy apartment was alive with the voices of from twenty to thirty neighborhood children. They huddled together on the living room floor and sat about on kitchen chairs listening attentively as Celestine and one of the Sisters explained the catechism to them. (Today, due in large part to the unselfish example Celestine had shown by providing these first quarters for the classes, there is a catechismal center in the neighborhood carrying on the work started in the Levy apartment.)

Late in 1937 the Levys suddenly faced a serious personal crisis. Their daughter was stricken with a kidney disease and it was feared that she would not survive.

"We took little Celestine to a convalescent home in upstate New York, and we prayed and hoped that with God's help and the good doctors she would pull through," Celestine recalls. "She fought for life bravely and showed great courage, and before long she was on the road to recovery. And as our daughter lay in the hospital near death Will and I thought that surely her terrible illness must be for some purposeful reason. And indeed it was, for it served to remind me once again of that promise I had made so many years before to Saint Joseph. God wanted us to keep that promise."

Thus, one warm day in 1938, Celestine and Will walked out of the New York Foundling Home with their first foster child, a cuddlesome, fifteen-month-old Puerto Rican child who would spend the next twelve years of her life under their loving care. From then on the Levy home was never without the laughter and joy of many children. Often they would be caring for as many as six youngsters, and when a permanent home was found for one foster child, the Levys would immediately apply for another child who needed a temporary family and the love the Levys were eager to provide.

Then came little Cathy. She was a Puerto Rican orphan who had come to the Levys when she was but six months old. At the age of three she was still with them since no permanent home had been found for her. For the Levys this was a blessing in disguise; they had grown very fond of the sweet-faced child and hoped that in some way they could keep Cathy for their very own always.

They filed the adoption papers for the child. Several tense months of waiting followed. They were now close to forty years old, the age limit for permanent adoption and they wondered if perhaps this would count against them. Then word came through. Cathy was theirs! Cathy is now a pretty eighteen-year-old and a fine student at Good Council College in White Plains, New York. The conscientious young lady earns most of her tuition money herself, and she hopes eventually to become a teacher.

Early in 1958 another permanent member was added to the growing Levy family. Will had embarked with his stepfather on a sentimental journey back to their ancestral Caribbean island home and it was here that Will came upon another child in need. She was a very thin, nine-year-old native child named Mariella. Her parents were dead and she was being cared for by her older sisters, but it was obvious to Will that the child needed real parents again. Will took one look at the cute, button-eyed youngster and immediately fell in love with her. He cabled Celestine and asked her what he should do. Back came the reply, "Bring her home."

"The little child took to American ways almost immediately," Celestine relates. "She broke through the language barrier very quickly, greatly aided by her teachers and a schoolmate, and she recently graduated from Holy Family School in New Rochelle."

The Levy's present home, on a quiet street in New Rochelle, was acquired on a part-ownership basis with the help of a relative of theirs. Soon after they moved in they became members of the Holy Family Church in their community and its pastor, Monsignor Charles E. Fitzgerald, became a good friend of the couple. One time he chanced to mention to them that a young foreign student then attending nearby Iona College was having some difficulty finding a place to live during the school term. The good father had no need to say more. "We'll help," the Levys replied exuberantly.

An extra bed was set up in the Levy home, and soon they were making room for other foreign students in need as well as for a number of American students from out of state. And when her own household was full to more than capacity Celestine canvassed her neighborhood and lined up other families, good people of all races and religions, each of whom would lend a hand in providing a comfortable temporary home for a student or two.

Since Celestine and Will are people of but average means these new additions to their family mean a further stretching of the household budget. "We don't mind this," Celestine says sincerely. "The students contribute what they can, and we're able to provide a good balanced diet for everyone by being alert to special sales on food and by keeping our own expenses down to the barest minimum."

This writer recently visited the Levy home, and in a matter of seconds I was made to feel like one of the closely knit family. Celestine's own daughter, her namesake, is married now and lives in Brooklyn, but as usual, the Levy house was overflowing with children and adults. There was Mariella, the Jamaican child, now a lovely young lady, and there was twenty-year-old Angie, who had come to stay with the Levys some five years ago and who had grown to love them both dearly. Also present at that time were three foreign students from the Caribbean island of Dominica, who were then the house guests of the Levys while they attended Iona College on scholarships provided for them by the Irish Christian Brothers. Another student, Victor Chow, from Hong Kong, was then doing his studying at the Levys and having his dinner with them. The house was seldom quiet during my visit as friends dropped in for brief chats with this very popular couple, and later in the evening all of us gathered around the organ in the living room to sing together harmoniously.

Will and Celestine speak pridefully but never boastfully of their "international" family. "We're not looking for praise for what we've done," Celestine says with the modesty that is so much a part of her character. "We're just grateful to God for all He's done for us in so many ways by letting us do something that we enjoy so much. What an empty life it would be for us if God in His goodness didn't continue to bless us as He has with children, even if they aren't our natural children. We're just very fortunate."

Celestine estimates that she and Will have been godparents to at least a hundred children over the years. This includes the offspring of several of their foster children who went forward from the solid upbringing the Levys gave them to take on the full responsibilities of adulthood.

Many of the Levy children are now scattered in different parts of the country and in foreign lands. Nevertheless, they keep a steady line of communication open with their "parents" via the mails. Several have worked their way through college or are now attending college. One of the foreign students they helped is now a teacher in his native Dominica, helping to raise the educational standards of his people; another is in Belgium continuing the medical studies he began in America so that he can help fight disease among his countrymen.

To all their children, no matter where they may be, Celestine is known as "Mom." There is one foster child of whom she speaks with very special fondness. The girl was fifteen when she came to live with the Levys. The family she had lived with previously had treated her with little affection and the experience had embittered the girl. "Don't think I'm going to ever call you Mom," the girl said sharply soon after she came to the Levys.

But as time passed the girl saw that life here was quite different from what she had known before. Sitting around the kitchen table with the whole family, laughing and joking with the other Levy "children," she soon realized that she was now part of a real family, that these were people who loved her and whom she could love.

"The girl is married now and has a child of her own," Celestine told me, and then added with a joyful smile, "I recently received a letter from her. It began, 'Dear Mom.'"

# XII

# They're Keeping
# Tom Dooley's Promises

On January 18, 1961, Dr. Tom Dooley, the courageous and greatly revered Navy doctor who had dedicated his life to healing the sick in the remote and primitive Asian lands that were beyond the reach of modern medicine, succumbed to cancer at the age of thirty-four.

The tragic loss was deeply felt throughout the world. In all the places that had been touched and uplifted by Tom Dooley's humanity there was now great sorrow at his passing; in the congested refugee camps on the edge of Red North Vietnam, where Dr. Tom had begun his devoted crusade to alleviate human suffering; in the native villages of war-ravaged Laos, where Tom had built his hospitals to minister to the sick; in the makeshift orphanage built in the thick Saigon jungle where Tom and the gentle, dark-haired Madame Ngai provided shelter for the countless orphans of war; and, most of all, his death brought sadness into the hearts of the millions of men, women, and children around the world who had only known the handsome, sparely-built humanitarian through his books, but who had been inspired by his great sacrifice to their own realization of the brotherhood of all men.

At eleven o'clock on the morning of January 23, the huge interior óf the St. Louis Cathedral in St. Louis, Missouri, was filled to overflowing for the pontifical Mass for Dr. Tom. A highlight of the solemn ceremonies was the reading by Father George Gottwald of several lines from a Robert Frost poem that Tom had loved so much:

> The woods are lovely, dark and deep.
> But I have promises to keep,
> And miles to go before I sleep,
> And miles to go before I sleep.

As the crowd of more than two thousand mourners filed silently out of the Cathedral, many of them repeated these lines over and over to themselves. "Promises to keep," Tom had said, and when death was near, still thinking solely of his work and not of himself, he had expressed the wish that his work "must always be a living, thriving thing for ever and ever." The mourners now wondered if a way could be found to "keep Tom's promises."

About nine months later a small meeting was held at the Mark Hopkins Hotel in San Francisco, California. Present were Tom's dear mother, his brother Malcolm, and several of the dedicated doctors who had worked with Tom at his jungle hospitals. On September 15, 1961, the results of this meeting were made public through an announcement by Mrs. Dooley of the creation of the Thomas A. Dooley Foundation, which would, in her words, "carry on Tom's ideals and work."

As Malcolm Dooley explains further, "We wanted to continue Tom's work in the way he would have wanted this done, on a direct people-to-people basis." As the father of seven fast-growing youngsters Malcolm has always had his hands full, but in spite of this he did manage to spend a year working with his brother and visiting the hospitals in southeast Asia. Back home he continued to help by spearheading fund-raising

Tom Dooley

drives for Tom. He is therefore very anxious to see Tom's important work continue. "It was Tom's idea that we should go right into the villages and live just as the natives live. In this way we would show them that Americans truly believe in freedom and human dignity for all peoples. Therefore, in establishing the Foundation, we set as our goal the creation of this people-to-people idea that Tom believed in so fervently."

The Foundation was to be nongovernmental, supported solely by public contributions. The initial work was to be in Asia, where the memory and admiration for Tom remained bright and where the need for aid was especially acute. The Foundation would send its people into an Asian country only at the request of the host government and with their full cooperation. Foundation teams would provide material assistance and spiritual example without doing so in a political package nor in any way interfering with the internal affairs of the country. Their object was the singularly important one of raising the health standards of the country through community medical programs and by training local personnel—looking forward to the day when the local people would be able to continue the work on their own.

The Foundation established its national headquarters at 442 Post Street in San Francisco, and then began to set up chapters in Monterey, California, Portland, Oregon, New York, and other cities. As the public began to learn of the Foundation's existence, thousands of letters from people in all walks of life started pouring into the national office, all asking just about the same question, "How can we help to carry on Dr. Tom's work?" And slowly Tom Dooley's promises began to be kept.

There was a time on a windy November day in 1960 when Tom stood atop a hillside and watched the grim lines of Tibetan refugees stream into northern India from their Red-besieged country. It was at that moment that Tom turned to the exiled Tibetan leader, the Dalai Lama, who was standing next to him, and assured him, "Help for these refugees will

Betty Moul, one of the first "Disc Girls," stops off at the Foundation-supported orphanage in Saigon on her way home from a trip to southeast Asia.

come from America. We will get the modern medical equipment that will ease the suffering of your people."

The Foundation's chapters are keeping this promise of Tom's. Working in a truly cooperative effort, the chapters have financed a fully equipped mobile health unit. One chapter raised the money to buy the jeep and trailer, the members of another chapter on Long Island contributed thousands of dollars' worth of medical and surgical supplies and the Monterey chapter collected the funds for the van.

On January 24, 1962, the bright new health unit, its sides carrying the signature of the thousands of people whose contributions, both big and small, had made this gift to the displaced Tibetans possible, arrived in Dharansola, in northern India. As it passed through the Indian village on its way to the refugee camp the Tibetans gave it a tumultuous welcome, garnering the van with scarfs, the Tibetan form of greeting. Dr. Melvin Casberg, a good friend of Tom's, who accompanied the van to the camp, said, "This was what Tom had wished for and prayed for. All of us connected with this project felt that we had now fulfilled our obligation to Tom."

It was in New York City that Tom spent much of his time when he was in the United States. There he raised funds and assembled medical teams to keep his work alive. It was natural, therefore, that the Foundation, in seeking to perpetuate Tom's deeds, would establish a very active chapter in New York and that an especially large role would be played in this chapter's activities by the woman Tom called his "good right hand," Teresa Gallagher.

From 1957 until his death, gentle-faced, twinkling-eyed Teresa Gallagher was Tom's volunteer secretary. It was she who organized "Tom Dooley's Disc Girls," the group of hardworking, dedicated young girls who handled the massive job of processing and replying to Tom's huge domestic and foreign correspondence. Tom would dictate his reply to each letter onto a recording disc, and the girls, most of them holding down full-time secretarial jobs, devoted much of their free time to typing the letters from the discs.

"The letters would come in by the thousands, but each one was answered," Teresa told this writer with considerable pride. Has the correspondence decreased since Tom's death? "Very little," Teresa answers. "You'd think Tom was still alive. We still receive offers of help from just about everywhere. A number of people, of course, found it very difficult at first to understand why God would take such a wonderful man as Tom away from us so soon. This was especially true of the youngsters who had read his books, and who had been inspired by Tom's example to pattern their lives after his. But now people understand that God must have had His reasons for taking Tom away from us, and that the important thing now is to continue his work."

"A number of the letters ask what steps can be taken to achieve sainthood for Tom," Teresa adds. "To these letters we reply by quoting Father Norman Pahl, O.M.I, who has told us that individual letters asking the Church to examine Tom's life, as well as any lists of signatures drawn up for this same purpose, should be forwarded to the Bishop of the place in which the person resides. The Bishops will then either forward these individual letters and petitions to Rome, or make a report to Rome on them."

Teresa's "Disc Girls" are still very much in the forefront of the effort to carry on Tom's work. Betty Moul, who was one of the first "Disc Girls," has toured southeast Asia several times. On her way back from one trip she stopped off at the Foundation-supported orphanage in Saigon. Here she found that the babies were being wrapped in burlaplike material because the orphanage couldn't afford to buy real diapers. The pretty young secretary made up her mind to get the diapers for the orphanage.

As soon as she returned to New York Betty picked up the classified telephone directory, turned to the listing of diaper companies, and started to call each one in turn. To each she related the plight of the orphanage babies and asked if they could help. The first few names she called said No, but Betty kept on dialing. Finally a diaper bleach company said they would supply the orphanage with fifty diapers for each of their 118 infants, and free of charge! "That's wonderful!" Betty shouted into the phone, overcome with excitement. The diapers were delivered to the orphanage and they were a welcome sight indeed to the hard-pressed staff.

One especially remarkable group now carrying on Tom's work is comprised of airline stewardesses who are sacrificing their vacation time and taking leaves of absence to go into the villages and hospitals of strife-torn southeast Asia to pitch in and help.

One such devoted young lady is Marleane Thompson. With her roommate, Margery Burgy, the attractive, blonde airline stewardess took an extended leave of absence from her job to journey to the Tibetan refugee camp in Darjeeling, India, to teach the refugee children English and introduce them to American songs and games.

It took them only a few days to pick up enough basic Tibetan to get by. Then the young girls set up their classroom right in the midst of the crowded camp. They started with a hundred pupils, but when word of the *Gey-Lhamoo-Lo* ("Angel Teachers") spread through the village, other children, as well as adults, jammed into the classroom to meet the "two pretty ladies who have come from a far-off land to help us."

When Marleane learned that the children had no combs she appointed herself their personal barber. "I cut their hair until my hands were sore, but I didn't mind at all," Marleane recalls pridefully. She and Margery also spent six days a week working at the Tom Dooley dispensary at the camp, in addition to running their classroom.

With a ten-dollar donation from an American tourist, Marleane bought some wool which the older girls in the camp used to knit some sixty pairs of socks, using needles made of bamboo. Since few of the youngsters had shoes, the socks came in very handy.

The two American girls picked up the Tibetan customs, and in turn taught the Tibetans some American customs. Theirs was a true person-to-person exchange, just the way Tom would have liked it. When they finally had to return to their jobs after four months at the camp, the girls promised that they would be back as soon as they could. They had worked wonders in showing the Tibetans that there are many "splendid Americans" like Tom Dooley willing to make personal sacrifices to help them.

Young boys and girls all over the world have organized "Little Dooley Clubs" and "Tom Dooley Memorial Clubs" to perpetuate the work of the man they so greatly admire. Teenagers at Notre Dame High School in Toronto, Canada, raised enough funds to buy a goodly supply of bandage strips, hypodermic needle sets, and baby nightgowns for the jungle hospitals, and at Christmas time they sent about fifty pounds of candy, toys, and nightgowns to the children in Laos. They accomplished this remarkable feat by taking any and all odd jobs they could find. They also raised $185 for the Foundation by holding a film program at their school and charging admission.

The youngsters in the seventh grade at St. Peter's School in New Brunswick, New Jersey, first learned about the noble life of Tom Dooley from their teacher, Sister Marie Peter, who read to them from Tom's books. The courage and unselfish devotion of the young doctor fired the imaginations of the children. "If one man can do so much good, think how much more good could be done if many other people joined in and helped," one youngster said to his classmates at the school. The other children agreed. They named their civics club in Tom's honor, and through his example they were spurred to a greater interest in science and medicine. "I couldn't tell the children enough about science after they had discovered Tom Dooley and taken him as their own," Sister Marie says. The youngsters took most of their precious allowance money and contributed the accumulated sum of thirty dollars to the Foundation.

Because of this heartening response from young people everywhere, the Foundation established its own "Tom Dooley League" to provide such youngsters with such help and guidance as they might need to put their interest and energies to work for the Foundation. The youngsters are advised that the Foundation would prefer that they earn the money themselves by taking on odd jobs, rather than by canvassing house to house or by soliciting by canister. This, the Foundation believes, will keep the activities of the youngsters as simple and direct as possible.

Tom's greatest wish was to see medical teams established all over the world so that disease can be eradicated forever. A big step in the realization of his inspired dream was taken just a short while ago when a Foundation medical team, at the request of the Royal Laotian government, arrived at the village of Ban Houei Sai in Laos to reopen the jungle hospital that had been started there by Tom. The team is now working with local medical people, training them and helping them care for the sick in the area.

As Malcolm Dooley concludes resolutely, "The Foundation is now doing what Tom first did, showing the people of Asia the warmth, sincerity, and compassion of America, and giving them new hope for the future. And to us at the Foundation this is but the beginning. The response we've received from thousands of people, young and old, rich and poor, has shown us that there are many who want to join us in carrying on all of Tom's work, and even more. A letter we received from a girl in Ontario, Canada, probably best sums up the feelings of all us now engaged in this important humanitarian endeavor. 'I thought that when Dr. Tom died everything went,' the girl wrote, and then added, 'But you have proven to me that he still lives and his candle is not snuffed out, it is still glowing, glowing very brightly indeed.'"

# XIII

# The "Miracle" Man of
# Speech Afflictions

THE BOY WAS a victim of asphasia, or total speechlessness. His mother brought him to the Holy Cross Speech Center in Brooklyn, New York. Here the child met A. Edmund Turner, the gently smiling, bespectacled, fifty-four-year-old speech therapist who runs this center and others throughout the city and in nearby New Jersey, all located in Catholic schools.

After Turner completed his examination of the boy, the mother asked hopefully, "Can you help my boy?"

"I don't know what I can do until I try," Turner replied sincerely. "If you are willing to bring him here every week for a lesson and faithfully do the daily exercises I prescribe at home —there may be great improvement."

The mother reflected for a moment. She was desperate. She could not get any guarantee that the boy would be helped. As Turner pointed out to her, "No professional person guarantees results; if he does, then he's unethical. All I can do is expose him to therapy that has helped thousands of other afflicted persons."

Thoughts raced through the mother's mind: I am a Catholic. This is a Catholic therapist who has been trained in Catholic

118

schools. Over 6,500 children and adults have come to this man. He did a marvelous job on my neighbor's boy. I am sure there will be no anti-Catholic suggestions in this therapy. He has trained many priests, seminarians, sisters, and brothers and has taught at Catholic colleges. Slowly a smile displaced the frown of anxiety on the mother's face. Yes, she too was willing to try.

Weeks of intensive exercises followed for the boy. Turner tossed restlessly in his sleep each night as he tried to think of some way he could make the boy's vocal cords produce some sound. Then he prayed. He asked God to give the little afflicted one the strength and courage to persevere in the exercises so that he could learn to speak normally.

There were several sessions with the boy and the prescribed exercises were constantly repeated. Still the boy could make no sound.

Then one afternoon the break came. The youngster made a great effort to move his lips. He summoned all his courage and strength and finally a sound came, a prolonged AHHH sound that descended in pitch.

Turner embraced the boy joyfully, then asked him to repeat the sound if he could. "Ah-h-h," the boy said again. "Now try it higher and then lower," Turner prodded him further.

The boy did it!

"We're on our way," Turner said happily to the mother standing nearby. "Now we can start on the mouth and lip formation to try to produce real words."

At the end of twelve lessons the boy had learned to say thirty words. For the first time he was able to say "Mamma."

"This is the happiest day of my life," his mother exclaimed joyfully.

Six months later the boy was able to speak complete sentences.

Was this a miracle? Turner answers only that it was a great good and all good things come from God. The science of speech therapy played a big part in the rehabilitation of this particular youngster, but constant, persevering prayer by both the parent and the therapist also played a major role. Only God knows which factor was the mightiest.

"The big sin in speech education," says Turner, "is the advice to do nothing. Usually speech defects explode, sometimes in childhood and most certainly in adolescence, into a major catastrophe in the afflicted person's life. The pent-up, speech-neglected child grows bitter, resentful, antisocial, and is easily drawn into delinquency." Turner is convinced that "if a child is not speaking normally by the time he is five, professional help should be sought."

Turner was graduated from St. John's College in 1933, after which he became a public speaking teacher. In 1941 he went into the Army and became an assistant adjutant at the Armed Forces Induction Center at Fort Bragg, North Carolina. While there Turner was shocked to see so many men in otherwise top physical and mental condition being rejected for their country's service, or assigned to menial tasks, because they had speech defects.

"What a waste," Turner mused. "Surely something can be done to combat this problem." Then and there he decided that it was more important to help these people than to teach normally speaking people how to talk persuasively.

In 1946, freshly mustered out of the service, Turner began to study speech therapy at Fordham University's School of Education. Two years later he was ready to put into practice all his stored-up ideas.

He felt that there should be well-trained speech teachers who would give full time and effort to Catholic schools. Though he himself had a permanent teacher's certificate in speech, enabling him to teach in the public schools of New York, he decided that he was more greatly needed and would be more useful to Catholic school children.

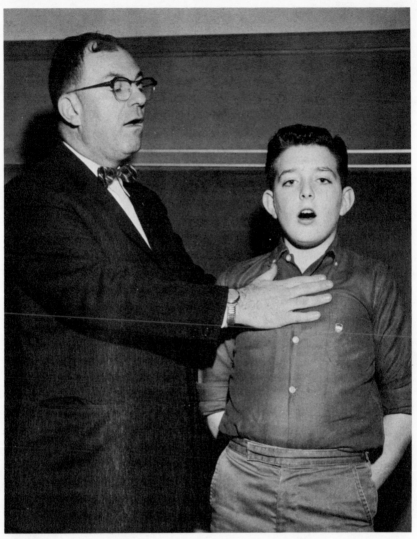

A. Edmund Turner with a student.

He presented his ideas to his friend Monsignor Joseph R. McLaughlin, then pastor of Our Lady Queen of Martyrs Church in Forest Hills, Long Island. The Monsignor gave Turner the use of the facilities at his school free of charge, as did the other six parish schools in which Turner subsequently established speech centers.

Early in October, 1948, the first speech correction center opened at Our Lady, and Turner officially launched his unique methods of speech therapy. These are based on Turner's belief that speech difficulties cause more psychological problems than psychological problems cause speech difficulties. He has taught hundreds of stutterers how to control their affliction. After the stutterers realize that they can talk in many speech situations where they were formerly hysterical mutes, their personality undergoes a complete change. Their self-confidence soars to new heights. Many have advanced to higher positions that were closed to them as stutterers. Corrected child stutterers have become public speakers.

A sixteen-year-old stutterer avoided all contact with people and never made friends. When she was walking on the street and passed people that she knew, she could only manage a hurried "hello," then rush on before they could engage her in conversation. Her mother heard of Turner's centers and brought her to a session. The stutterer does not breathe properly, control pitch and volume, or speak at a normal rate, Turner has found. "If the stutterer can learn to control these three factors," he says, "he or she can usually learn to speak normally."

Turner put his heart and soul into the task of helping this teen-age girl. He first sought to reduce her tensions and fears by giving her relaxation exercises. Then he taught her how to breathe diaphragmatically, how to control a descending pitch, and how to control volume and her rate of speech.

Recently this very girl stood up in front of a group of parents and children gathered for a center session and delivered a two-minute speech she had prepared for her biology class at school. She spoke without any trace of the stuttering that had previously caused her so much shame and suffering. Under Turner's patient direction, she has won a new lease on life. In fact, she recently volunteered to serve as a teacher in a religious vacation school.

One afternoon not long ago this writer visited one of Professor Turner's centers. Turner has no staff, and no help of any kind. He personally teaches every student in his centers. Each student receives an individual lesson. At present he is giving over 175 lessons every week.

The centers are open to people of all faiths. However, each speech-defective child must be accompanied by a parent. This is one of Turner's cardinal rules.

"Each weekday lesson given at the center is practiced twice a day at home by both the child and the parent," Turner pointed out to me. "The mother is the first, God-given teacher of every child. Just show her what to do and she will outdistance any strange teacher by miles."

I watched Turner begin a lesson with a little girl. The child's mother sat nearby, a notebook and pencil in her hand. Turner placed a wooden depressor against the girl's tongue. With the fingers of his other hand he gently shaped the child's lips into the right speech position. "Say *Kay,* darling, say *Kay,*" he urged the child.

"Gay . . . Gay," the girl managed to utter. She was having great difficulty pronouncing the K sound. Her mother watched as the teacher showed her how to place the depressor in the girl's mouth and how to form the lips so the girl could enunciate K.

Intently watching the process was the audience of other speech-defective children, each accompanied by his or her mother. Turner believes that by having all his students and parents watch each case being handled they are inspired and challenged to work that much harder on overcoming their own speech problems.

"You're doing fine, dear," Turner encouraged the little girl. He always speaks to the children in soft, fatherly tones, praising them when they are almost at the point of success, spurring them on, and vigorously instilling in them hope and courage.

"Try to say *Kay*," Turner continued to prod the child, as he gently pinched her nostrils to prevent the escape of air.

Finally the child managed to say *Kay—Kay*. It was the first time in five years that she had been able to master the *K* sound.

Turner took the child into his arms and kissed her. "You did it, darling, you *did* it!" The child smiled at him happily, and kissed him full on his cheek.

Each lesson takes no more than fifteen minutes. This is about as much instruction as a child can handle each time. Then the mother follows up what she and the child have learned at the lesson by repeating the training each day at home until the next session.

A little boy comes up next. When he was first brought to the center he was having great trouble pronouncing the TH sound. Now, after eight lessons, he has overcome his speech difficulty.

"Say your Hail Mary," Turner says to the youngster.

The boy repeats the prayer distinctly.

Turner often uses the Hail Mary as part of his lessons. He has found that the prayer's familiar words come easily to the patient because the child doesn't have to stop to gather his thoughts. But even more than this, the prayer has been a great source of inspiration to both therapist and patient. "It has helped see us through many a seemingly hopeless case," Turner affirms.

Turner has no waiting list for his centers, nor does he ever ask anyone to attend. He prefers that people come without special urging, out of their own great desire and interest in seeking his help.

Two evenings a week, Turner also conducts centers for speech-defective adults. A visitor to one of his evening classes can see a good cross section of people from all walks of life—a housewife, a bricklayer, a bacteriologist, office workers, even a young man hoping to enter a seminary when his speech defects are cleared up. Each one must also be accompanied by a friend or relative who will follow through on the training with them between sessions.

One man, seventy-one years old, had been a stutterer all his life. Nothing he had tried on his own had helped him overcome his handicap.

He practiced Turner's exercises faithfully each day. The professor's encouragement and confidence sparked him on to make this great new effort to conquer his life-long affliction. At the completion of his thirteenth lesson he walked confidently into a paint store and, without any hesitation, said to one of the clerks, "Let me have a half pint of turpentine." Never before had he been able to say the word *turpentine*. Now he spoke it clearly and without faltering. He went back to the store almost every day for several weeks after that; each time he ordered another can of turpentine, until his apartment was almost filled with the stuff. It was just one word out of many that he could now say for the first time.

Another patient, twenty-one years old, had a serious stuttering problem, which had kept him from his heart's desire—to become an Army officer. After completing twelve lessons at one of Turner's centers he was able to obtain a re-examination. He passed it unqualifiedly.

He came to Turner and announced the good news. As he shook the therapist's hand he said, "Thank you very much." His words of gratitude were spoken without any trace of his former speech impediment. Turner smiled pridefully. He had spent many a restless night on this case, but now he had received the only reward he is seeking in his work—the joy and satisfaction of knowing he has helped another afflicted human being end his suffering and begin a new, useful life.

## XIV

# The Boxing Champ
# Who Became an Altar Boy

On a warm afternoon in New York the auditorium of one of
the city high schools was alive with the buzz of young voices.
Suddenly the teen-agers—all of them journalism students at
the school—stopped talking among themselves as their attention was attracted by a man making his way to the apron of
the auditorium stage. "I'm Tommy Loughran," the man introduced himself.

Back in the Golden Twenties Tommy had held the title of
world's light-heavyweight boxing champion and had been considered a model of Christian living. Now in his fifties, Tommy
is still solidly built and in top condition, his black hair is
greying only slightly, his face is still fair-complexioned and
unscarred. He walks with the erect, self-assured movements that
show him to be still a champion.

"All of us are instruments in God's hands," he said in a
gentle, persuasive voice to the gathering of youngsters. "Most
of us will never do anything really earthshaking, but just about
all of us can do something worthwhile in our lives if we just
do the best we can. All of you are studying to be writers. I
have a suggestion for you. When you go out to write a story

127

about a sports event, don't write about the big star of the match, the one everyone is watching and cheering for. Look around and find a little guy, an inconspicuous figure who's out there trying with all his heart to do the best he can to help his team win. He's the guy you should write about."

Tommy might well have been thinking of himself when he passed on this sound advice to these teen-agers, for his own life has always been based on doing something worthwhile, the best way he could.

As a boy in a poor section of Philadelphia Tommy early realized that he had a natural inclination toward boxing. So he set himself the task of becoming a professional.

He turned the basement of the modest Loughran home into his own special gym. He covered the walls with mirrors, and when he wasn't out taking care of his newspaper route he was down in the basement shadowboxing for hours at a time. He'd crank up an old phonograph and box rhythmically to fast music. Each record played for about two and a half minutes, just about the time of a prizefight round.

One of his neighbors, Joe Smith, was familiar with the intricacies of the fight game. One afternoon he visited the Loughran home and stood awhile watching Tommy work out. "I can probably get your boy a couple of fights," Joe said to Mrs. Loughran, who wanted her son to follow through on his boxing interest, confident that he would only do the right thing. So Tommy began to fight in amateur bouts and also, of course, to continue the religious training that was an equally important part of his life. At sixteen he became a communicant at St. Monica's Catholic Church, a small parish in his Philadelphia neighborhood. In the years to follow, Tommy won some thirty-five bouts. Growing into young manhood he perfected his fighting skill, concentrating on outsmarting and outmaneuvering his opponents rather than by outpunching them. Fight managers would often remark that Tommy "looks more like an altar boy than a fighter." As Tommy explained it to me when I spoke to him a short while ago, "I've always considered the body to be the temple of the Holy Ghost. The body should always be kept in good condition and never thought of as something just for personal vanity and self-pride. Rather, the body should be treated with respect and should never be abused."

Tommy adhered strongly to his faith. He became known as a "clean-living" fighter; he never smoked, drank, or went night-clubbing, and he attended Mass regularly at St. Monica's. As Tommy told me, "I knew quite a few other fighters who also attended Mass regularly and lived by high moral standards. Unfortunately, this isn't publicized or played up very much by the newspapers and sports writers."

Tommy fought the best of them—Gene Tunney, Harry Greb, Mike McTigue—and in 1927 he realized his boyhood dream: he became light-heavyweight champion of the world.

When retirement came some ten years later, Tommy could say that he had always carried himself with dignity and humility before God, that he bore no moral scars. A short time later Tommy came to New York's fabled financial district, Wall Street, to work as a broker for a sugar company. It was here that Tommy, then in his mid-forties, really became an *altar boy!*

He learned that a new Catholic church, to be named Our Lady of Victory, was being built near his Wall Street office, and that the fathers needed some help with their ritualistic duties. So Tommy became one of the first members of the church's force of volunteers. And with the church's Monsignor Richard J. Pigott, a tall, genial man, he found a mutual interest—the fight game. "I'm certainly glad to meet you, Tommy," Monsignor Pigott told him. "I'm a boxing fan myself and I followed your career very closely." (The two boxing enthusiasts are now close friends and often get together to reminisce about the "good old days" of prizefighting.)

Tommy also agreed to serve during Wednesday Mass when the church was first opened. "It was something I'd always wanted to do when I was a boy," Tommy explained to me. "Also, I wanted to show the young boys that there's nothing unmanly about being an altar boy."

The red-brick, modest-sized church was completed in 1946, and its services today exemplify a unique "democracy of the altar." The faithful come in large numbers—businessmen and office workers from the many office buildings that surround the church—to spend part of their lunch hour in prayer and meditation in the quiet of the chapel. It is very usual to see a successful businessman and several of his employees kneeling together, side by side, one before God.

Tommy attends service at Our Lady every day. As one of the fathers told me, "Tommy is a wonderful Catholic and an inspiring example for young people."

Using his own religion-centered boyhood as his guide, Tommy has developed a keen understanding of the "growing pains" experienced by young people. "Young people need to be treated with kindness and patience," says Tommy. "They should be encouraged to keep themselves in good physical and mental condition through regular exercise."

"To me, exercise has always been a form of prayer," Tommy goes on to say. "It's an ideal way of keeping undesirable tensions from building up in young people. Exercise gives them a healthy release from pent-up emotions and the fatigue a youngster feels after a vigorous workout has a wonderful, settling effect on his mind and spirit. I've seen quite a few problem boys change for the better through regular exercise, and I'm convinced that this is a good way to lessen juvenile delinquency."

Tommy travels all over the country and spends at least one evening a week speaking before youth groups and civic betterment organizations, advising teen-agers and adults to lead what he calls "the good, religious life."

A worried father came to Tommy one afternoon. He was having serious difficulty with his teen-aged son. "I'd like my boy to be a lawyer," the father said, "but he insists he wants a career in professional sports."

Tommy went to see the youngster. His calm, easy manner immediately won the boy's friendship. "Remember that your father loves you and wants only the best for you," Tommy said. The boy was adamant about wanting to be in professional sports. Tommy spent a little while with the youngster, talking over his ambitions with him and watching him work out.

"I can see that your boy doesn't have that exceptional talent one must have to get anywhere in the very crowded fight game," Tommy said privately to the father. "But if we tell him now to quit and forget his idea he'll just become stronger in his feelings. It has been God's design to give young boys a great deal of energy and to make them unpredictable and somewhat rebellious. Yet it is also amazing how, if we are patient and understanding with them, they will work out their lives in the right way."

"Yes, you're right, Tommy," the father agreed. "Sometimes we do get a little impatient with them and try to force them to go along certain lines that we feel are right for them. I won't try to make him do what he doesn't want to do."

Some time later the boy, now a maturing young man, visited Tommy at his home. He himself had now realized that he was not suited for a professional sports career, and he was soon to enter the legal profession. The two men shook hands. "The handshake is all they have to say," Tommy told me. "Then I know I've helped them."

A short while ago Tommy was in the dingy cellar headquarters of a teen-age gang, which had been in some trouble with the police for petty crimes. The young, black-jacketed boys gathered admiringly around the strapping ex-fighter. "I'd like to challenge your leader," Tommy said. "I don't know who he is but I'd like to dare him to do the things he's been telling all of you to do." Tommy's voice rose to a defiant pitch. "I think your leader is a coward. He'll suggest bad things for all of you to do but he won't do them himself. All of you will get in trouble, but he'll be in the clear. I say your leader is a fake. Will he accept my challenge?"

The young faces turned to look at one husky boy in the crowd. The boy's eyes were downcast. He made no move to speak. Tommy's challenge had shown him up and broken his power over the gang. The boys surged forward to shake the champ's hand and from their respectful handclasps Tommy knew he had won another round for God.

"If we all lived by the Ten Commandments the world would be a much better place," Tommy concludes in sincere affirmation of his lifelong faith.

# XV

# Adelaide Helps Change
# the World

THE FIVE O'CLOCK rush was on. The sweating, pushing, gum-chewing crowd of subway riders was jammed into one of New York City's BMT subway trains as it roared through the dark tunnel. Suddenly a young man looked up from the folded newspaper he had been reading. His eyes darted upward, toward a black-and-white placard posted high up on the side-wall of the subway car. It was one of an even row of car cards which advertised such products as toothpaste, chewing gum, soft drinks, and a dozen or so others. The man stared at this card, and a perplexed, searching expression lined his face. It was like no other subway advertising card he had ever seen. It heralded no product; it was merely a simple but impressive listing of the Ten Commandments. Along the bottom of the ad was the cryptic statement THIS SPACE PAID FOR BY A FRIEND. Unconsciously, the man began to repeat the Commandments slowly to himself. Other passengers also spotted the strange "ad" and they too began to read it over silently.

Who was the "Friend" responsible for this unique, God-loving idea? This was what reporters from the local newspapers wanted to know. They pursued the hunt vigorously, and after some dogged legwork they finally tracked down the anonymous "advertiser." It turned out to be a forty-eight-year-old Brooklyn woman, Adelaide O'Mara. Asked what had impelled her to pay for the posting of such an unusual ad card, the cherubic, redheaded stenographer replied with deep conviction, "It's been my dream for many years. I thought it might do some good."

Having such a notice posted in subway trains is quite expensive—$400 a month, a sizable sum for a working girl to scrape together. Adelaide had to save it up dollar by dollar, over several years. She scrimped quite a bit, often going without that new dress she craved or that new pair of shoes, putting the money instead into her "Ten Commandments Fund." And when she received a handsome bonus from her employer for her thirty years of service in this one firm a good chunk of the money went right into the "Fund."

Finally Adelaide had the necessary amount. She rushed down to the office of the subway advertising company and purchased space for 1,250 car cards, to run for one month. The salesman who sold her the space was so deeply moved by her unselfish deed that he donated his commission from the transaction to a worthy religious charity. She told only her mother and a few friends what she had done, since she was not looking for personal glory or praise.

How many actually saw the ad? "At least a million," Adelaide estimates with a happy smile. She remembers how, sandwiched in among sophisticated New Yorkers on their way to work, she would check, noting how many passengers glanced at the card and reflectively read the age-old words of guidance. She then knew that the fulfillment of her dream was bringing comfort and new resolution to many.

Adelaide hopes that others will follow her example and take on similar projects to bring people closer to God. As she says, glowing with unquenchable faith, "I've heard it said that sometimes even a small thing can change the world."

Adelaide O'Mara inspects one of her subway posters.

# XVI

# Where Labor and Management Meet

OUR LORD's last words to His disciples and their successors, to go forth and teach men "all things whatsoever I have commanded you," are being advanced today from within an unpretentious four-story brick building on West 16th Street, in the midst of New York City's sprawling industrial network. Here a dedicated group of Jesuit priests have maintained the highly praised Xavier Institute of Industrial Relations, where rank-and-file union members are taught "to help themselves and then to help others."

The Institute was a Depression baby. American workingmen, caught in the economic holocaust of the thirties, were turning in increasing numbers to extremist panaceas and to "pie-in-the-sky" social theories. Convinced that Catholic social teachings held the answer, Father John La Farge and a group of other priests and lay Catholics met, on a February afternoon in 1936, in a small room in Xavier High School at 30 West 16th Street. This was the first of more than a dozen such meetings stretching over the next several weeks, from which would finally emerge the plans for the launchng of the Institute on this site.

At first it seemed as though the Institute were doomed to

failure. Labor people looked upon it with misunderstanding and suspicion. "It's just a strikebreaking cover for management," they said. At the same time management viewed the Institute as a pro-labor, anti-management front.

Groundwork for the great task of winning the confidence and cooperation of both labor and management was laid, during these first formative years, by devoted Jesuits like the Reverend Philip Dobson and the Reverend Joseph P. Fitzpatrick, the school's first directors, who carefully perfected the Institute's curriculum and proved that the school had the best interests of labor *and* management at heart.

In June, 1940, came the appointment of the Reverend Philip A. Carey as director of the Institute. Father Carey is an idealistic Jesuit who was to have a great influence in shaping the school's future. He is imbued with a deep understanding of people, a determination to mold human nature for the greater good, and a firm desire to improve labor-management relations through Catholic social teachings.

Born in the Bronx, New York, in 1907, he was the son of a trolley motorman who had to work seventy to one hundred hours a week for meager wages and under the worst possible working conditions. His family's early difficulties and privation instilled in the young boy a sharp awareness of the working-man's desperate need to improve his lot and of the important part played by strong, democratic labor unions and enlightened management in this struggle. Young Philip went to the Jesuit college in Woodstock, Maryland, and was ordained in 1938.

"To my way of thinking, there is only one way possible to win the worker," says Father Carey. "Through sympathy. And I mean sympathy in the real meaning of the word, 'suffering with.' It means putting yourself in the other fellow's boots. If the fellow in the shop sees that you're sincerely interested in the good of the workers, he'll be on your side."

To put his principles into action, Father Carey has joined

the men in their meeting halls, employment offices, and factories. No "company man" he, but no anti-management man either. Rather, he is approaching industrial problems in the oldest of Catholic traditions: inspired by the example of Our Lord, the worker, the carpenter, fighting the exploitation of labor and teaching cooperation among all men.

"The priest must sell the idea to the workingman that work is a vocation, sanctified. The priest has to present the need of cooperation among workers after the ideal of the Mystical Body of Christ. The workers know what cooperation is and what it means. The ideal of the Mystical Body, of which he is a member, gives the worker something to live for and to work for. It gives new meaning to his life."

Working men and women, truck drivers, telephone girls, oil workers, office clerks, auto workers, members of a hundred different types of unions are today enrolling at Xavier, and management too has enlisted its support. Tuition at the school is only $5, and this is waived for those who can't afford it. The intensive, two-year, one-night-a-week study includes classes in labor law, trade union methods, economics, parliamentary procedure, labor ethics, contract negotiations and the job of the union officer.

To the union men trained at Xavier, dedication to the betterment of their lives and the lives of all workingmen are cardinal principles.

There was the young paper worker who served as shop steward in his plant. Devoted to his men, while at the same time realizing that the "boss" also has his problems which must be considered, he had made his plant one of the best-run, most cooperative all-around factories in the trade.

Then his brother-in-law asked him to leave the plant and go into private business with him. Should he now leave the men who were dependent on his leadership and the rapport he had established between labor and management?

Father Carey and students.

"The whole thing comes down to this," he said anxiously to Father Carey in one of many friendly talks he had with the Xavier director. "When the whole thing's over and Saint Peter is making the introduction to the good Lord, I wonder how I'd want it to be done. Would I like Saint Peter to say, 'Lord, here's Pete, the rich businessman,' or would it be maybe better to hear him say, '. . . Pete, the paper worker'?"

"You've had the training, Pete; answer it for yourself," Father Carey said. (The entire staff at Xavier follows the rule of making suggestions when called for, but never actually telling anyone what to do. Any definite action must be decided by the men themselves, impelled by their own sincere feeling that this is the right thing to do to benefit their co-workers.)

Pete chose to stay at the plant. His training at Xavier had shown him how he could best serve others and now his life was dedicated to putting the Institute's principles into effect. And even when Pete was offered an executive job at the plant he turned it down, deciding that he was worth more to everybody as shop steward for his union.

In 1946, a tall, ruddy-faced Irish priest, Father John M. Corridan, was assigned to Xavier as Father Carey's assistant. The congested Hudson River waterfront is only a few blocks from the school, and each day longshoremen streamed in and out of Father Corridan's office to tell him fearfully of the racketeers and corrupt union officials who held the livelihoods and the very lives of the men under constant threat. Father Corridan listened with rising indignation as the men told him of the evil shape-up system by which workers were hired each day only if they pleased the corrupt officials. The job of cleaning up the New York waterfront was enormous but Father Corridan undertook it with fearless resolve. As one newspaperman described him, "The father is as cool as a cucumber, as patient as Job, and as tough as the situation demands."

He amassed tons of data on the deplorable dock situation,

A Mass of thanksgiving at the completion of the third tube of the Lincoln Tunnel in New York. Father Philip A. Carey is celebrant.

then wrote and spoke about what he had uncovered in news-papers and on radio and television. He found writers and jour-nalists who wanted to help him. He spoke to other union men and to the shipping company executives. "The cause of the men of the docks, the hard-muscled, honorable men whose work means so much to our daily living, is a challenging call to all Christians," he cried out passionately. "For these men are our brothers, redeemed in the precious blood of Christ, and one cannot rest secure if His dignity in them continues to be violated and outraged."

State and federal investigations of the appalling waterfront jungle came in the wake of Father Corridan's mighty crusade. Significant reforms have been instituted to bring greater de-mocracy within the local longshoremen's unions and a fair system of hiring is being developed to replace the shape-up. Today Father Corridan is teaching theology in New Jersey, behind him now the good fight he fought and won to uphold "the dignity of man."

From his compact but comfortable office at Xavier, Father Carey maintains a tight schedule of activity. The sturdy, white-haired, fifty-five-year-old Jesuit is spiritual advisor to hun-dreds of workers. He is often called upon to bless a union's new headquarters or to lend a hand in some difficult labor-management dispute.

"All labor-management problems are moral problems," Fa-ther Carey maintains. "Neither Communists nor racketeers can stand democracy. Every union leader who sticks to what is best for his union, his industry and his nation is going to defeat any of those elements that rise in his organization."

To this end Xavier's faculty teaches its students to "recognize the fact that a union has responsibilities as well as rights, and that management also has rights as well as obligations."

A unique part of the school's program is its "Grievance Clinic." A hypothetical grievance is outlined for the class, then the students are divided into teams of ten management and ten union representatives. Working under the guidance of an experienced mediator, the teams draw up their strategy and arguments and then set about mediating the grievance over the bargaining table. The sessions are often heated as the students are thoroughly grounded in everything that goes into an actual labor-management arbitration session. At the next session, the teams are switched and the same procedure is followed. In this way the students learn at first hand how it feels on both sides of a labor-management dispute and arbitration and a greater understanding of and sympathy toward the problems and viewpoints of both is engendered.

Father Carey and his faculty can now look with pride to the school's more than eight thousand graduates, men who are today among the nation's leading and most highly respected labor leaders, including Joseph A. Fisher, international president of the Utility Workers Union, Joseph Denny, international president of the Brotherhood of Book Binders, and John J. Dillon, educational director of the United Auto Workers Union.

"The Xavier Institute has been a strong and steady light, helping men to see the meaning of their actions in the perspective of eternity; helping them to judge their human purpose against the divine plan for justice among men," says Father Joseph P. Fitzpatrick, the school's second director, now on the faculty of Fordham University. "Commitment to the obligations of organized activity, competence, conscience, these are the symbols of Xavier's greatness in the past; they are the promise of Xavier's greatness in the future."

# XVII

# Wheels for Our Lady

THE MIDDLE-AGED woman, bedridden for the past fourteen years and unable to use her vocal powers, was on the train that was taking her to New York, where she would continue by fast liner her arduous journey to Our Lady's Shrine at Lourdes. Her family's financial help had made this long and expensive trip possible, but as she rested on her stretcher, her nurse beside her, she couldn't yet know of the crisis that would soon befall her, or of the courageous men and women whose unselfish actions would bring her through it triumphantly.

Her transportation arrangements had been made by a Chicago travel agency and it had seemed that everything would go smoothly. Then a message suddenly came through to the agency: the ship's doctor, because of the serious physical condition of the woman, had declined to accept the medical statement certifying her ability to make the trip. Without his approval, she could not sail on the ship.

With the woman still en route to New York and as yet unaware of the serious complication that had arisen, the agency people had to move fast. "The Wheels will do it," they said, and a long-distance call was hastily put through to the office of the New York City Fire Department's Bureau of Civil Defense and its head, Captain Joseph Reilly. Joe Reilly is the director of "Wheels for Our Lady," a volunteer organization of Catholic laity, both men and women, dedicated to helping the lame and the sick who pass through this big metropolis on pilgrimage to religious shrines in Europe.

"Here's the situation, Joe," the travel agency man explained. When he was through speaking, Joe simply replied, "We'll take care of it."

Joe then made a few phone calls of his own, first to Marion Murphy (another Wheel) and then to several other members. They were all there with Joe when the train pulled into New York's Pennsylvania Station. Removing a car window they eased the stretchered woman into a waiting ambulance and took her to a nearby Catholic hospital to be cared for while arrangements for a change in transportation were started. While the woman rested from her long train ride, Marion made plane reservations for her. She would leave that day on a 7:00 P.M. flight. The doctor at the hospital granted her a medical certificate, citing the great faith and courage she had shown in her unswerving desire to reach Lourdes.

Early that afternoon the ambulance took Joe, Marion, and the woman through the crowded streets, then on to Kennedy International Airport where the woman was gently lifted into the airport nursery, where she could comfortably await her departure time.

It was a few minutes before four o'clock. The woman suddenly began to feel severe pain. While Marion stayed to comfort the woman, Joe rushed into the office of the airport authority and blurted out, "We need a doctor. One of our people is in serious pain." The great work of the Wheels was well known to the airport people. "We'll get the airport doctor," they said quickly.

The airport doctor was in the midst of applying a cast to a

patient. He was immediately summoned. He rushed into the nursery coatless, his hands still covered with plaster of Paris, and acted to relieve the woman's pain. Meanwhile, airport employees were busy with their own plan to help the courageous traveler. An airport worker came into the nursery with a broad smile and told Joe, "We've got a place on the four o'clock flight. She won't have to wait until seven."

The woman was strapped carefully to a stretcher and the gentle hands of the Wheels raised her to a standing position so she could be gotten around to the berths in the giant plane. The woman smiled warmly at all those who had helped her, and as the plane soared into the clear, midafternoon sky Joe and Marion stood at the gate with a prayer on their lips for her safe journey.

She was but one of hundreds of pilgrims who have been helped by the men and women of Wheels for Our Lady, an organization that has no officers and no treasury, one that is completely motivated by the spiritual fervor of its members.

It began a few years ago with one woman who had been on a tour of Europe. Returning to the United States with a group of pilgrims who had visited Lourdes, the woman saw at first hand the difficulties these people had to surmount in getting transportation from the airport to local hotels, or to trains and buses that would take them home. These difficulties were especially harrowing for those confined to wheelchairs.

"Can't something be done about it?" the woman said to her friend Marion Murphy (Mrs. Gerald P. Murphy), a dedicated Catholic Actionist.

"We should have some kind of organization to help overcome these problems for these handicapped pilgrims while they're passing through New York," replied Mrs. Murphy.

It was May—the month of Mary—and in a Catholic newspaper, Marion noticed a picture of Joe Reilly and the statement that he was president of the Firemen's Holy Name

Society and very active in Catholic lay affairs. "Perhaps he can help us find the people for such an organization," she thought.

In a telephone call she explained her idea to him. Captain Reilly, fifty-one, is a veteran of twenty-six years in the New York Fire Department. A white-haired, stockily built, gently smiling man, Joe holds a cherished place in the Department's Honor League for saving the life of another fireman. The father of three, Joe has himself been to Lourdes and well knows the great power of the Shrine to the sick and the afflicted.

"The idea sounds wonderful," Joe told Marion Murphy enthusiastically. "I'll speak to our chaplain, Monsignor Farley, about it immediately, and to others in the Department." Everyone Joe spoke to responded in favor of the idea, and inside of a month, with Joe and Marion directing the operation, the Wheels were put into motion.

"We hope that our movement will stimulate interest in the making of pilgrimages to Our Lady's shrines by showing even the most seriously afflicted that they can make such a journey and that we will help them do so," Captain Reilly told me. "We help pilgrims to hotels, to morning mass, and to all the modes of transportation they have to use on the long and arduous trip."

Volunteer Wheels now comprise some thirty-five men, mainly from the city's Fire, Police, and Sanitation Departments (because they have access to the equipment needed) and some fifteen Catholic lay women. "We never actually go out to recruit people," Captain Reilly further told me. "We prefer that people come to us out of their own deep desire to help others."

Marion Murphy expressed her own feeling that the response of people to the Wheels idea is "the greatest expression of brotherly love I have ever witnessed. Even in pouring rain or heavy snow the people come out to help these pilgrims. They take an intense and personal interest in the comfort and well-being of God's afflicted ones. It is a demonstration of the virtue of charity never to be forgotten."

The nineteen-year-old boy, paralyzed as a result of a spine injury, was on his way back by plane to the United States, after a nine-day pilgrimage to Lourdes. Midway in the flight the boy became seriously ill. A doctor traveling with the group of pilgrims warned, "There's danger of pneumonia setting in." The pilot immediately radioed ahead for help. "Get in touch with the Wheels," he added.

Captain Reilly was called and quickly apprised of the emergency situation. "I'll take care of it," Joe said. He immediately called a local hospital and asked that an ambulance be sent to the airport to meet the plane. And he himself was there when the plane taxied in. He moved in to help in taking the sick boy from the plane and to the waiting ambulance to be taken to the hospital for treatment. "We've come to know that the Wheels are ready for any emergency," an airport employee told me.

In addition, the group's gentle concern for the pilgrims has been a source of inspiration to everyone they have come in contact with. A short while ago an ambulance driver at a New York hospital was assigned to drive one of the pilgrims to the airport. Captain Reilly and Marion Murphy went along. At first the driver looked on it as just a routine assignment, all part of a tough job, but as he moved slowly through the streets, giving the handicapped woman inside as comfortable a ride as possible, the driver found a kinship with the Wheels and an understanding of the needful work they were doing. When he returned to the hospital a few hours later, after having delivered his passengers to the airport, the driver immediately went to his superior and asked, "Anytime the Wheels want someone to drive one of their pilgrims to the airport, please give me the job. If I'm not working at the time then call me at home. I still want to do it, even if it's on my own time."

Bill Spinelli has been with the New York Fire Department for some twenty-six years. His family of eleven children keeps him mighty busy, but he still finds time to be an active Wheel. "I've derived a great deal of spiritual gain by helping these afflicted people and by giving them hope and making it possible for them to go to Lourdes."

Recently, Bill received an important promotion in the Fire Department. He told me, "It was my own work and also my prayers and the prayers of these people that I've been privileged to help that really did it."

Tom Hoarty, a member of the New York Police Department, and his wife consider their Wheel activity an important part of their Catholic action. To them it is a "devotion to the Blessed Mother, to whom we owe so much. The work isn't a duty, it's a pleasure. The faith and courage of these people have given us a great lift and made us feel stronger."

Madeline Slattery is an advertising executive and she provides some of the "woman's touch" to the Wheels. "The bravery of these people so impressed me that I went to Lourdes myself," Madeline told me, and then added, cheerfully, "It's nice to do things for people."

Any afflicted pilgrim can contact Captain Reilly at his home address (89 Seaman Avenue, New York, N.Y. 10034). The usual procedure is for the pilgrim to arrange his regular travel details with a travel agency, and then have the agent contact the Wheels, telling them just what kind of equipment will be needed (stretcher, wheelchair), also the manner of transportation into New York and the time of arrival. The Wheels are ready to handle not only individual pilgrims but also group pilgrimages of ninety or more people.

Just before they are to leave for Lourdes, the pilgrims spend some comforting moments within the calm and majestic confines of the Chapel of Our Lady of the Skies at Kennedy International Airport, where they take part in special departure ceremonies and receive the Pilgrim's Cross, the Benediction of the Most Blessed Sacrament, and the Blessing of the Sick. And they know that it was a small, devoted group of Catholic men and women who made it possible for them to be on their way to Lourdes.

As Marion Murphy said to me, "The Wheels are Mary's gift to her handicapped children. The organization developed almost of its own accord. The sincere, enthusiastic response by those approached for participation, the cooperation of everyone involved, can only be termed 'heaven-sent,' or shall we say 'Mary-sent'?"

# XVIII

# Saint Bruno in the Slums

IT IS EARLY morning, almost any morning, on East 9th Street in New York City. On the doorstep of a tenement building a group of Puerto Rican youngsters are huddled around the figure of a slight, sandy-haired, thirty-three-year-old man. The man is teaching them the catechism. The boys listen quietly, their small faces intense with concentration. Occasionally one of the boys breaks in and asks the man, whom they all affectionately call "Mr. Pat," a question. The man answers carefully and clearly, then continues the lesson.

"Mr. Pat" is Irish-born Patrick M. J. Moloney, and this "sidewalk study group" in religion is part of his own personal mission to the people of New York's poverty-racked Lower East Side. From this building Moloney operates his "Bonitas Youth Service," an inspired humanitarian work utilizing the goodness of all men.

Pat Moloney knew this same kind of poverty in his own childhood, spent in County Limerick, Ireland. His father was a carpenter with seven children to care for as best he could. Often the family had to go without necessities, but they found comfort and nourishment in the love of God and a sense of good-

151

ness that could weather all hardships. While still a boy Pat set his heart on entering the priesthood. He received his high-school education from the kindly and devoted Trappists at Mount St. Joseph Abbey, in Roserea, County Tipperary. It was while studying with the Trappists that young Pat first learned about the Order of the Carthusians and of their devotion to the goodness of man. He made a vow then that some day he would visit one of their monasteries and learn more about their exalted way of life.

One summer day in 1953 Pat, then twenty years old, stood before the high, majestic walls of the St. Hughes Charterhouse of the Carthusians, nestled in the still woodlands of Sussex in the south of England. On the side of one of the walls was carved the word BONITAS, the Latin word for "goodness" and the favorite expression of Saint Bruno.

"Then and there I realized that this meant the goodness of Almighty God and of everything He has created," Pat now recalls. "It meant the divine spark of goodness that is in everything and in every human being."

In April, 1955, Pat came to the United States to pursue his studies for the priesthood. He entered St. Mary's Seminary in Baltimore, Maryland. At the end of his first semester he decided he wanted to enter the Charterhouse of the Carthusians, set in the quiet, snow-blanketed hills near Whitingham, Vermont. "Perhaps you should first finish your studies for the secular priesthood, and then let God guide you from there," the superior at the Charterhouse advised him. Pat agreed. He enrolled at St. John's University in New York. While studying he also held a job as a counselor in a Brooklyn children's institution in order to build up some savings.

In the section of Brooklyn in which he found a place to live he also saw his first opportunity to help others. He observed how during the summer the city children had to play on the congested and often dangerous streets of the neighborhood.

How much better it would be, he contemplated, if these children could spend their summer days at a beach.

With his first few months' savings and with the money he had planned to use to pay for a trip back to Ireland to visit his mother, he bought himself a second-hand station wagon.

Every weekend a crowd of youngsters from the neighborhood would pile into the car and Pat would drive them to a nearby beach and camping area.

He taught the youngsters how to live in the outdoors and to take in fully all the grandeur of nature. He bought pup tents for them himself, going from one cut-rate store to another to find the best buy he could within his small resources.

In January of 1958 he moved to East 9th Street in Manhattan because of the lower rents in that area. This was his first encounter with an American slum neighborhood. All around him he saw grimy, rat-infested tenement buildings squeezed together on garbage-strewn streets and inhabited by desperately deprived, mostly Puerto Rican families. Here too he witnessed the exploitation and injustice that fed on poverty.

Most of all he saw the results of these conditions: families being torn apart, the children hungry, often having to go for days without any food, the adults turning to alcoholism and drug addiction as futile escapes from their hopeless environment.

"I made friends with the youngsters and started taking them to the beach on weekends," Pat remembers. "And I talked with them often for hours at a time. They wanted something more out of life—and they were willing to work for it. Within them I was sure was the divine spark of goodness that Saint Bruno had spoken of, if only these youngsters could have the opportunity to fulfill their capabilities."

"And as I learned more about the terrible plight of these youngsters I thought about the ideals of Father Flanagan," Pat adds. "That's what I've believed in all of my life. There's no such thing as a bad boy, if he can be shown that someone cares, and if someone tries to understand him. I realized that these kids simply want a place they can refer to, where they can feel of some use, where they're recognized as individuals. In the streets they're of less value, less importance, than the automobiles driving by. They feel in the way, in the midst of a cold, indifferent, impersonal city. As impersonal as the sea. And as cruel."

Word about the kindly, friendly young stranger in the neighborhood soon spread around and the people of the section, children and adults, began coming to him for help and advice on their problems. Overnight he became a leader in the fight for decent living conditions in the neighborhood. One day he'd be fighting a Puerto Rican family's battle against a landlord who had refused to clean up the unsanitary conditions in a building. Another day he'd be in court pleading for one of his "boys" who had gotten into trouble with the law. Still another day he'd be leading a protest against a local merchant who was cheating and swindling some of the poorly informed Puerto Rican families. He'd even be called upon to handle the arrangements for the baptism of a Puerto Rican child.

It all became so complicated that Moloney decided he had to have a definite place to work from. He found such a place in a narrow, unpainted store at 713 East 9th Street, a block away from where he lived. His studies for the priesthood were temporarily set aside so he could give his full heart and mind to what he now called "The Bonitas Youth Service." His only outside activity was a part-time job, from which he could earn the $45 a month rent for the store.

"We started out with no funds at all," Pat says. "That's the miracle and mystery of it. We've managed to scrape along somehow without any, depending instead on divine providence."

One day, shortly after he had opened the store, Pat was

passing the Convent of the Franciscan Missionaries of Mary on 45th Street. He decided to go in and explain his predicament to the sisters. Every weekend thereafter he received from the sisters all the food he could carry—leftover items from the nearby food chain, including bread, damaged canned goods, powdered milk, and sometimes candy. Pat also canvassed the neighborhood groceries and bakeries and got assurances from them that they would turn over their surplus food to him. It soon became a regular event each morning for the youngsters of the neighborhood to appear in front of the Bonitas Youth Service and carry away with them the precious bread, lard, and other supplies that their families so desperately needed.

Soon the little store itself began to take shape. A separate room was set up, with a library of books that Pat himself accumulated for his boys. And a little kitchen. The boys scoured the neighborhood looking for salvageable junk that they themselves could repair and make serviceable again. They took on any odd jobs that were offered them, using the money they received to help their families, and even giving some of their earnings to the Service. "The boys weren't afraid of any kind of work," Pat states. "I remember one time an elderly lady, confined to a wheelchair, called us up and asked if we could find someone who would wheel her around while she did her shopping. I thought for sure we'd have trouble getting any one of the boys to do this. They'll think it's a sissy job, I said to myself, but as soon as I told them about it they all volunteered without hesitation."

By now one hundred and fifty boys of the neighborhood, ranging in age from five to seventeen, were "Mr. Pat's assistants" at the Youth Service. And adults volunteered to help as well.

One volunteer helper Pat is especially proud of—an elderly man living in the neighborhood. One afternoon he came into the store. "I want to distribute some bread to the poor families

on Sixth Street," he said. Pat had heard stories about the man.
He had a reputation in the neighborhood for being shiftless
and untrustworthy. "Don't give him any bread. He'll just sell
it and keep the money for himself," several neighborhood
people had told him. But Pat remembered the words that had
first inspired him to begin this personal mission—"the divine
spark of goodness in all men."

He loaded the man down with loaves of bread and directed
him to the homes of the people who needed food so badly. A
few hours later the man returned to the store. His arms were
empty. "I gave out all the bread," the man said, smiling warmly.
"It was tough work but it sure felt good." Later investigation
substantiated the fact that the bread had been distributed free
to the families, just as Pat had believed it would be.

In the yard behind the store Pat had a continuing accumulation of furniture and other odds and ends, donated by his
friends and by those who had heard of the Youth Service by
word of mouth or through publicity in the local newspapers.
The boys would spruce up the discarded pieces, repairing and
repainting the furniture until it was in the best possible shape.
Then Pat would canvass the area to find out who was in the
greatest need of the type of furniture available.

"It was truly heartening to see the spirit of goodness evi-
denced in these people," Pat says. "I would visit a family that
I knew was using a very old, broken-down bed, and I would
tell them that I had a good bed for them that someone had
donated to us. They would say with great emotion that they
would like the bed very much, but there is another family,
one floor down. They have no bed at all. Please give it to
them, they would say, we'll wait for the next one."

The goodness that Pat has found in people extends well
beyond the confines of his neighborhood. Margaret Marchant, a
gentle-faced diminutive woman in her sixties, works as a clerk
in a charity thrift shop. Pat would come into the shop several

times a week to inquire for low-priced camping equipment for the boys. Before very long Margaret was putting articles aside for him.

One day Pat heard that Miss Marchant was planning to repaint and redecorate her apartment. "You've been so good to us, Margaret," Pat said to her on his next visit to the store, "that the boys have volunteered to help paint your apartment for free."

For the next five days the Youth Service boys labored pridefully for about ten hours a day. They wallpapered two rooms, painted the doors and windows and did all the plastering necessary. When they were finished it was a job worthy of professionals.

A few days later Miss Marchant held a party for the boys in her shining bright apartment. Margaret's sister Agnes was present, as was Pat. Midway through the evening Agnes suddenly said, "You know, Pat, we have an old house in New Jersey. We've owned it for twenty-five years. But we haven't even seen it for years and it's in need of a great deal of repair. Do you think perhaps you and the boys could put it into some kind of livable shape? Then you can use it as a place for summer vacations. You can have the house for nothing if you want it."

Pat could hardly believe it. An actual summer place for his boys! Why, he'd dreamed of getting such a place but never in his most fanciful imaginings had he ever believed he'd be able to get together enough funds to buy such a house. Now it was being offered to him free and clear. "We'll drive out there Saturday," he said, his voice choked with excitement. "It sounds wonderful."

On a clear June day in 1960 the Youth Service station wagon pulled up by a heavily wooded area near the Musconetcong River, in New Hampton, a small New Jersey town. Pat and the boys piled out. "The house is over there," Pat indicated its location with his hand. The group made its way through the thick overgrowth of bushes surrounding the house. Finally they sighted the place itself. It was a two-story house dating back to the Civil War days, its rickety frame surrounded by five and a half acres of rugged land covered with wild growth. The house was in a seriously dilapidated condition. Extensive repair work was needed. Yet, as he stood there with the boys and looked up at the weather-beaten front of the house Pat could only say, "It looks like a palace."

The boys swept the floors of the house, cleaned the windows, and made enough makeshift repairs so that they could all move right in that very night. That summer the boys, who had only known the stifling atmosphere of slum living, spent their days swimming and camping, making the house over from top to bottom, settling under the shade of a tree to discuss religion with Pat, safe and happy in the healthful splendor of the country.

But some of the people in New Hampton resented the presence of Puerto Rican and Negro youngsters in the vicinity. Ugly incidents occurred. Twice, when the boys were swimming in the river, people from the town approached them and warned them to "get out of Hampton!" The house was also broken into and ransacked.

"I told the boys that some people didn't understand the meaning of democracy," Pat says. "I told them that these people weren't evil or cruel, but only lacking in human understanding."

During the next spring, on the night of May 23, 1961, the house was empty. Soon it would be summer again, and back in teeming Manhattan Pat and the boys were looking forward to returning to their own special place. That night, a sudden crackling sound was heard in New Hampton, and in a matter of minutes the old wooden frame of the house was engulfed by a fiercely spreading fire.

A few hours later the phone in the Youth Service office rang. It was a friendly local resident calling to tell Pat what had happened. By the time he arrived the house was nothing but charred and smoldering debris. Whether the fire was the result of an accident or arson is still unknown.

"God sometimes gives with one hand and then takes away with the other," Pat explained to the sad-faced boys he had taken with him to the ruins to help him salvage whatever he could. Then he added hopefully, "Maybe He wants to give back with *both* hands."

A few weeks went by. Pat was in the store busily helping a needy family. He answered the ringing of the phone on his desk. Mr. and Mrs. Anton Joas, a young New Hampton couple who had been friendly to the boys, were calling to offer the use of their barn for a working party of older boys. "At least the land can be cleared this summer so that it can be used by the boys for camping purposes," they suggested.

A few days later a New York woman phoned the store and said she would like to help with the rebuilding. "Are you a welfare worker?" Pat inquired cordially, after thanking her for her offer. "No," the woman replied. "I'm an attorney by profession, and I am also a human being who believes I'm my brother's keeper."

"God gives back with both hands," Pat had said to his boys, and subsequent events have borne out his inspired words. With the help of the Catholic Charities of New York Pat has been able to send a good number of his boys to summer camps, and a short while ago, bolstered by the donations of a number of supporters, Pat was able to move from the store into a six-story building at 606 East 9th Street, which he and his staff of adult volunteers have turned into a home for homeless boys. The door of what is now known as Bonitas House is always open for any homeless boy from sixteen to twenty-one. Here the boys live and work and grow strong in body and soul.

And Pat adds fervently, "Some day something great will rise on the site of the old house that burned to the ground. I think we will see there some day a Youth Town where boys from the city slums will be taught skills that will enable them to put their talents to the greatest and most worthwhile use. With God's goodness and man's goodness I am sure it will all come about."

# XIX

# *The Courageous Young Men of ACTU*

THE PUERTO RICAN woman had been forced to work for sub-standard wages . . . The muscular, middle-aged longshoreman was being harassed by racketeers who had taken over his union . . . The young woman had a serious work grievance that both her union and her employer had refused to correct.

Where could they turn for help? The union members knew at once. They went to the always-busy office of the New York chapter of the Association of Catholic Trade Unionists (ACTU), located on the third floor of an inconspicuous gray building at 327 Lexington Avenue. Here ACTU's staff, composed of courageous, religiously inspired young Catholics, was ready to help them, as it has aided thousands of other trade union members in their struggle for better working conditions and social justice.

For more than twenty-five years union members have recognized ACTU as an organization always ready to fight for their best interests. ACTU was born on the afternoon of February 27, 1937. Some eleven men and women, all of them trade unionists except for one who was a lawyer, gathered that day for an informal meeting around a kitchen table in the then

161

*Catholic Worker* building in a run-down section of New York's Lower East Side.

All those present at the meeting were Catholics who were deeply concerned that the then young, but rapidly growing, American trade union movement should not fall prey to corrupt and subversive influences, but grow and mature under democratic principles.

The young unionists recalled the words of Pope Pius XI, who had urged that, "side by side . . . with unions, there should always be associations zealously engaged in imbuing and informing their members in the teaching of religion and morality, so that they in turn may be able to permeate unions with that good spirit which should direct them in all their activities."

The result of the meeting was the forming of just such an association, which, in the years following its inception, would have a significant effect for good on the course and development of the entire American labor movement.

From the start, the founders of ACTU made it clear that the association would not be a "Catholic clique" in the labor movement that aimed to gain control of unions for any secret or questionable purposes. "We hold no threat to union leaders except such as work for selfish or subversive aims," they emphasized. "We need stir no alarm in industrial management that is forward-looking, fair, and democratic." Rather, ACTU sought only the justified rights of all workingmen: their right to wages sufficient to support their families in reasonable comfort, to hours and working conditions in accord with human dignity, to be able to bargain collectively through free and democratically chosen union representatives, and the right to strike and picket peacefully for a just cause. At the same time ACTU stressed the obligation of the worker to do an honest day's work for an honest day's pay, to refrain from violence, to respect property, and to abide by legitimate agreements.

*Charles Harbutt*

Dan Schulder of ACTU discusses labor-management practices with Puerto Rican workers.

ACTU members join teachers in picketing for better working conditions.

In November of 1937 ACTU began to put its ideas into concerted action. The Association opened a labor school in Brooklyn, where it offered, free of charge, to rank-and-file trade unionists of all faiths comprehensive courses on union practices, parliamentary procedure, labor law and grievance processing, and trade union ethics. The courses were designed to educate the worker in his rights and responsibilities so that he could instill these democratic principles into every operation of his union. (A number of ACTU labor school graduates are today in the top rank of the American labor movement, including Joseph Beirne, president of the Communications Workers of America, AFL-CIO, and Joseph Kane, vice-president of the American Bakery and Confectionery Workers of America, AFL-CIO.)

The Association's ranks were soon swelled by workers, professional people, students, and housewives. Together they helped to organize unions, walked in picket lines, took part in union rallies, and, in 1938, launched the first Catholic labor publication in America, *The Labor Leader*.

In the fall of 1940 ACTU became a nationwide organization, with chapters in key cities throughout the country.

The year 1947 saw the first major test of the organization's influence for good. That year the labor movement was rocked by disclosures of the wholesale take-over of a number of unions by avowed Communists. Local 144 of the Building Service Employees International Union, representing the workers in some two hundred New York hotels, was controlled by Communists, who were using the union for political purposes. The hotel owners, seeking labor peace at any price, were cooperating with the Red unionists who had "sold out" their members by obtaining contracts for them that afforded them fewer benefits and lower wages than other hotel workers were receiving.

Peter Ottley, a young Negro union official, joined the ACTU members in the local in a vigorous attempt to unseat the

Communist leadership of the union. They were careful, however, to make sure that their fight didn't serve to destroy the union itself. Their object was to get the Catholic members of the local to participate more actively in the union, and to present programs to the entire membership that were better than the programs offered by the Communists.

Ottley and an aroused members' committee, with the aid of ACTU, formed a democratic caucus in the union. They distributed leaflets and petitions calling for the election of new leaders, not necessarily Catholic, who would not subordinate the union's true functions for political gain. Their fight reached a successful climax with the election of democratic, anti-Communist leaders, who loosened the Red grip on the hotel industry and ushered in better working conditions for the hotel workers.

Similar fights were conducted by ACTU, in combination with other organizations and government agencies, against other Red-dominated unions, and in time the Communists were purged from labor's house.

But now racketeers and other corrupt influences moved in for their own take-over of the American labor movement.

The gangster-dominated International Longshoremen's Association ruled the New York waterfront with bullets and intimidation. The racketeers and shipowners had joined in an "unholy alliance" that had turned the docks into a veritable jungle. The dock workers themselves were being broken in body and spirit by the evil shape-up system, under which only workers favored by the racketeers who ruled them could secure work.

John Dwyer and John Mullins, both dock hands and ACTU members, helped start a reform movement on the waterfront, together with Father John Corridan, S.J., the famous "Waterfront Priest." The racketeers struck back by expelling Mullins from his local and making it almost impossible for him to earn a livelihood on the docks. But Mullins wouldn't be bullied or pressured into submission. As with all ACTU members, he had the courage of his convictions.

In 1953, on the strength of evidence compiled by ACTU members like Mullins and Dwyer and by other organizations working to clean up the docks, the AFL expelled the ILA from its ranks. Almost simultaneously the Bi-State Waterfront Commission of New York and New Jersey was created. The Commission's investigation resulted in the enactment of legislation making it illegal for a felon to hold office in any of ILA's locals, and also modifying the infamous shape-up system. A strike vote now had to be taken democratically among each local's members, and the union in general had to become more responsive to the best interests of its members. In 1959, a somewhat reformed ILA was accepted back into what had then become the AFL-CIO.

One day a middle-aged Puerto Rican woman visited ACTU's New York office. Dan Schulder, then secretary-treasurer of the chapter, listened to the woman as she described the intolerable conditions that existed at the factory where she worked.

"The young girls who paint the dolls—their faces break out and they'll never get married," the woman said in a heavy Spanish accent. "No babies—nothing."

The Puerto Rican workers in the factory had to paint faces on dolls, using stencil pencils. The women then cleaned up their work with a chemical solvent that caused their skin to break out. Protests by the women to both their employer and their union brought no remedial action.

Dan Schulder investigated and discovered an appalling situation. The union that was supposed to be representing the workers in this toy factory was little more than a dues-collecting racket. The workers had not even seen the contract that they had supposedly signed with their employer. All they received in return for their dues was low pay and long hours of work.

Schulder, a former semi-pro football player and warehouse

worker, stormed into the office of the union and laid the grievances of the workers squarely in the laps of the apathetic union
officials. The union was compelled to take action, or face a
protest strike by the workers. They made the employer change
the chemical solvent to one that wouldn't cause skin rashes,
and even more, they began to take steps to improve the overall working conditions at the factory, including the wages and
hours of work.

ACTU found that this wasn't an isolated case. New York
was literally infested with "dummy" and racket unions, which
worked in collusion with corrupt employers to exploit thousands of Puerto Rican and Negro workers.

The exploitation started because small, marginal businesses
in the city wanted to get a competitive advantage in their
industry. They found they could do this by paying the lowest
possible wages. In this way they could undercut their com-
petitors' prices. But to do this they first had to prevent legitimate unions from gaining representation for their employees and
obtaining decent wages and working conditions for them. This
was where the racket unions entered the sordid picture. They
offered the employer a "sweetheart contract," under which he
only had to pay his workers a few dollars more than the minimum wage. In return the union guaranteed the employer
"labor peace" and complete control of his business whereby he
could do whatever he wished. For this deal the employer would
pay off the union officials and also collect dues from the workers
to further enrich the union racketeers. Without bothering to
consult the workers at all, the union and their employer
together drew up their contract. Then, after the contract was
already set, the employer would go to his workers and tell them
they had to join that particular union. Anyone who refused
was fired. With the contract signed and sealed and the workers
delivered, the shop was now, under the NLRB ruling, closed
to organizing by any other union.

Day after day members of the racketeer-controlled International Jewelry Workers Union filed into ACTU's office to plead for help in changing the vicious conditions under which they were forced to work.

ACTU members Norman de Weaver, Ed McGuire, John McNiff and Dan Schulder began secretly to gather data on this racket union to be presented to law enforcement officers and the AFL-CIO Ethical Practices Committee. In the open, ACTU placed all its legal machinery at the disposal of the workers to help them break the "sweetheart contract" that controlled their working lives. ACTU members went from shop to shop, educating the workers in their rights and encouraging them to fight for these rights within the union and to demand respect from their employers. In a number of cases the workers had to resort to strikes to start the wheels of justice moving, and ACTU members were right there with them on the picket lines.

In 1957 John McNiff testified before the McClellan Committee on Improper Activities in the Labor or Management Field and made public all the shocking, heavily documented evidence of exploitation and corruption that ACTU had gathered on the racket unions operating in New York.

As a result, the Ethical Practices Committee of the AFL-CIO began an intensive investigation of the Jewelry Workers Union. At the same time New York state and city authorities also began to move. New York County District Attorney Frank Hogan seized the union's books. Its international secretary, Hyman Powell, was arrested and indicted on fourteen counts of conspiracy, grand larceny, and forgery. Powell eventually pleaded guilty and received a prison term.

The AFL-CIO placed the union under a monitorship, and at its 1959 convention a reform ticket, backed by ACTU, was elected to begin a sweeping clean-up of the union. The old "sweetheart contract" was scrapped and new agreements were drawn up, based on terms that were fair and equitable to both the union's members and their employers.

ACTU's racket-busting activity resulted in the passage of a New York State labor-management practices act, under which all unions are required to file reports on their finances and which made illegal many of the domineering practices of the racket unions. In New York City, a Mayor's Committee on Exploitation was created as a public watchdog against the racket unions. (Jim Ryan, former president of ACTU's New York chapter, is a staff member of the Committee, and another former ACTU official, John Conlon, is now an assistant to the Commissioner of Labor of the City of New York.)

ACTU realized that a major reason for the growth of the racket unions was the language difficulties encountered by the Puerto Rican workers and their consequent lack of knowledge about American union practices and their rights and responsibilities. ACTU therefore opened a Spanish-language labor school at the Nativity Church on New York City's Lower East Side, the first such school in the country. Spanish-speaking teachers were recruited from the ranks of the Puerto Rican workers themselves to conduct classes that would cover the entire field of labor union activity and the rights of the workingman. Each evening Puerto Rican workers crowded into the classrooms and came away armed with new educational weapons with which to better their working conditions.

One Puerto Rican worker who had tried to get action on the work grievances of himself and his fellow workers was continuously rebuffed by both his employer and his union's officers. He heard of ACTU's Spanish-speaking labor school and began to attend the classes faithfully. Upon completion of the courses, and now fortified with a complete understanding of intricate labor-management practices, the man pressed his fight with renewed confidence and determination. He went straight to the officers of his union, and backing his case with his newly acquired knowledge, insisted that the grievances of the workers be heard and acted upon. A short while later the man had the prideful satisfaction of seeing the grievances corrected.

Some six thousand Puerto Rican workers have received training to date at the four ACTU Spanish-speaking labor schools situated at key points in the Metropolitan New York area. In addition, many thousands of other workers have been trained at the association's regular labor schools.

Such have been the achievement-filled years of ACTU's activities. Essentially, ACTU combats the enemies of labor by working to improve the labor movement itself. In this way the organization encourages both labor and management to assume more responsible attitudes toward each other. The Association acts as a vital information belt on union corruption and racketeering, enabling state, city, and federal agencies to transform ACTU's findings into laws to protect the rights of workers and their unions.

Though continuously hampered by limited funds (a short while ago they had to suspend publication of *The Labor Leader* because of low finances), ACTU continues to fight the good fight, doing God's work to bring a just and democratic social order to all men.

# XX

# Faith Behind the Footlights

In a small, cozy former lecture hall on West 57th Street in New York City a mighty link is being forged today between the pulpit and the theater. This is the home of The Black-friars' Guild, the unique and highly influential Catholic experimental theater conducted by valiant priests on a completely nonsectarian basis. For more than twenty-five years these kindly fathers have labored diligently to fashion what they have termed "a theater of beauty and truth." They have traveled a rocky road to reach this goal.

Back in 1931 there was no such theater group, but there was an idea in the fertile minds of two priests: wiry, resourceful Father Thomas Carey and his friend, stocky and agile Father Urban Nagle. Both men were deeply interested in the theater. Father Nagle, in fact, was an accomplished playwright, who continued to write plays until his death in 1965.

They decided that the nation's capital was an ideal place in which to found a little theater movement where they could, as they put it, "present plays that *should* be presented instead of merely criticizing the ones that shouldn't have been."

They chose the name Blackfriars because of its religious significance. In England in 1576 many of the works of Shakespeare and Jonson were performed at a former religious home of the Dominican Fathers. The Dominicans were also called the Black Friars and so the home was dubbed the Blackfriars' Theater. The name is indeed apt for a modern-day theater designed to reflect Christian truths.

The fathers began a long trek through the city of Washington to find a suitable home for the Blackfriars. They visited just about every vacant building until they came upon a well-built, imposing structure attached to St. Dominic's Church. They advertized for help and many of the local amateur and professional actors volunteered their services. They also doubled as carpenters and electricians. Looking back on those hectic early days, Father Carey now recalls: "I don't know how we ever managed to get the place in shape. We had to stretch every penny; even our monthly allowances went down the drain. Father Nagle and I were able to give the venture only what idle moments we could spare. Before long, however, we were thinking, worrying, and praying theater."

On a clear, calm evening in March of 1932 the lights went up on the first Blackfriars' production, Father Nagle's play *Barter*. Some Washingtonians came and their reactions were complimentary. *Barter* had a short run and at its closing there was a small profit. But there were some people in Washington in 1932 who argued that an alignment between the Church and the stage wasn't proper. They brought pressure to bear and the fathers had to leave St. Dominic's and begin again a search for new quarters.

The Blackfriars traveled around the city, putting on makeshift productions wherever they could find a welcome. Once they put up their sets in a former bakery; another time they set up their theater in a vacant garage. Sometimes parish halls were temporarily made available to them. They built up a steady and faithful audience and soon the idea caught on in

other cities. In a few years there were eighteen active Blackfriar chapters in the country.

In 1937 Father Carey and his venturesome troupe were
invited to Catholic University in Washington, D. C., to create
a Blackfriars Institute of Dramatic Arts for the college students.
Father Carey applied his energy to this new task. He visited
the offices of several New York producers, "Won't you help
us?" he pleaded. From them he begged and borrowed truck-
loads of used equipment for the Institute. Catholic University's
Department of Speech and Drama, which Father Carey organized, is today a world-famous center of religious theater activity.
But Father Carey knew that this was just a short respite; the
real Blackfriars' work must go far beyond the University
grounds. So, leaving one of his assistants in charge of the
Institute, he and Father Nagle struck out once again.

In the summer of 1939 the Blackfriars founded a summer
theater at Nabnassett, Massachusetts. They had no money and
for two months the troupe lived on little more than peanut
butter and tomatoes. The venture was a dismal failure and in
addition the chapters in the other cities were now almost completely inactive. It looked like the end of the Blackfriars' idea!

On a summer afternoon in 1941 the fathers arrived in New
York, where they'd been assigned to regular church work. They
stood on a bustling Manhattan street corner and Father Nagle
said resolutely, "Look, we're here. We haven't quite done it
yet. This is the place!"

So another trek began to find a new home for the Blackfriars. After weeks of wearisome searching, a place was found
in the back of a huge business building at 316 West 57th
Street. But the fathers discovered that finding a home was just
the beginning.

Father Nagle hurried to the license office of the Fire Department and was told that first he had to obtain a license from
the Department of Public Events. There he was stopped by a

smiling, conscientious clerk, who advised, "Of course, you must get a certificate of occupancy from the Department of Buildings. If you make any changes in the place you must apply to the Board of Standards and Appeals. By the way, have you seen the Commissioner of Licenses?" No, he hadn't, but he was going to. Before the week was up he was to visit dozens of license offices before he cut through all the administrative red tape needed to open a new theater in New York.

Then Father Carey and several of his friends rolled up their sleeves for the task of turning an unimpressive lecture hall into a comfortable theater. Working almost day and night, they built a proscenium and a lighting switchboard. Father Carey visited the site of the New York World's Fair, which had closed a short while before, and for a little money he bought up a good supply of left-over lumber, electrical equipment, and drapery. The hall's wooden chairs were changed to soft, upholstered seats. The fathers and their volunteer helpers scrubbed the stage and swept the floors. Finally the sign could be posted outside the theater; the Blackfriars' curtain was going up.

The first production in this building, on an October evening in 1941, was Sean Vincent's Irish comedy *Up the Rebels*. It lasted just four nights and only one regular drama critic attended, but the comments from those who did come were encouraging. The fathers mustered together all their meager resources and fashioned a second production, Felix Doherty's soulful dramatization of the life of the celebrated English poet Francis Thompson, *Song Out of Sorrow*. But misfortune again plagued the good fathers. The play opened on December 11, Pearl Harbor week, and no one was interested in seeing a religious play. The fathers gazed dejectedly at their empty theater and empty treasury. "We need at least five hundred dollars to keep going," they agreed. That day Father Carey drew up a sizable list of prominent New Yorkers. He visited each of them. He explained exactly what the Blackfriars were trying to do and why there was an important need for such a theater. After some polite refusals, he found a donor, a charitable New York businessman, who handed the father a check for $500—"to continue your great work," he said sincerely.

The Blackfriars were back in business. In April of 1942 they presented Father Nagle's *Savonarola*. New Yorkers by now were flocking to the little off-Broadway theater and drama critics from all the New York papers began to review its productions.

Today the young priests carrying on the mission of Father Carey and Father Nagle thoroughly read the hundreds of playscripts sent them by aspiring writers from all parts of the world. They seek plays that have artistic merit, and that express positive values. They avoid plays that are superficially religious. "Catholic theater, like Catholic life, is not an eternally adolescent thing built entirely on sweetness and light," they emphasize. "The plays may discuss philosophy, science, temptation, and sin, and the characters with whom the audience sympathetically identifies must solve their problems according to the basic teachings of the Church and not give scandal in the process."

The Blackfriars have put on over forty-one productions. Many of these plays were written by non-Catholics. Some of them have delved into the lives of Church saints, but many others have been concerned in a straightforward manner with contemporary problems, racial prejudice, politics, morality.

The audiences are predominantly Catholic, yet many non-Catholics are regular Blackfriar patrons. One production was Father Nagle's *City of Kings*, a glowing dramatization of the life of Blessed Martin de Porres, a Negro saint. The production drew an especially large audience of Negroes, many of whom were non-Catholics. Seeing this heartfelt tribute to a great

Negro was a deeply moving experience for the Negro theater-goer. Several of them were so impressed by the play that they later became converts.

The actors contribute their talent in exchange for this excellent opportunity to enhance their acting abilities and perhaps to be seen by theatrical producers, many of whom regularly attend Blackfriar productions. Some seventy-five performers who appeared early in their careers at Blackfriars are today steadily employed in the professional theater. The alumni includes such famous names as Geraldine Page, Darren McGaven, Pat Breslin, and Dennis Patrick. Playwrights Robert Anderson and Louis Peterson had early works of theirs performed by the Blackfriars.

Casting for the plays is completely nonsectarian; in fact, most of the actors who have appeared have been non-Catholics, several even non-Christian. Yet they always bring loving attention, firm belief, and true devotion to their roles. Their devotion often goes far beyond the plays in which they appear. To them, the fathers are more than employers; they are also good friends. Often an actor will draw one of the fathers over to one side to share a problem with some ever-attentive priest. "I'd like your advice, Father," the actor will say, for he knows that the fathers can always be counted on for help and guidance. There is no chasm here between religion and the theater; each is here to help the other.

There was a highly successful Broadway producer who paid regular visits to the Blackfriars' office. One afternoon the producer and several of the fathers were deeply engrossed in a conversation about the overabundance of obscenity in some main-stem shows. "Is it all really necessary?" one priest asked sincerely. This set the producer to doing some serious thinking.

A short while later the producer was at a party celebrating the out-of-town opening of his latest play. He was overheard saying to a group of his friends, "I'm wondering if all the obscenity in the play is really worthwhile. I think it might improve the play from the standpoint of good taste and artistic merit if we took out a good deal of it." The cuts were made and everyone concerned with the production agreed that the changes vastly improved the value of the play.

The Blackfriars are now firmly rooted in New York, but there are still problems. When new owners took over the building they refused to renew the Blackfriars' lease. The fathers began to search again for a new home. They visited warehouses, churches, empty lofts, but no other suitable place was available. Then the School of Radio Technic, which then had its headquarters in the building, obtained a long-term lease on the theater for its own use. The radio school officials heard about the plight of the Blackfriars. "We believe in your group and what you're trying to do," the school officials said. "Won't you stay on under our lease?"

Thus another crisis was passed and the Blackfriars began their great, spiritually uplifting work again. "The final, serene, and humbling gratification of our years on the boards is to know that none of this would have been possible without our audience, our critics, and our friends," they conclude resolutely. "God bless all of them!"

## XXI

# To Fill the Church's
# Greatest Need

THERE IS NO question that the Church's greatest need right now is to fill the void created by the shortage of priests, nuns, and brothers so the Church can move forward from the Ecumenical Council with full strength.

How serious is the present shortage? Joseph Cardinal Pizzardo, Prefect of the Sacred Congregation of Seminaries and Universities, estimates that the 228,000 Catholic priests in the world are only about half the number needed to minister adequately to the spiritual needs of the world's 418,000,000 Catholics.

The problem is equally critical in the United States. Father Godfrey Poage, C.P., executive secretary of the Pontifical Work for Religious Vocations, says: "In the United States alone the number of priests and nuns must be doubled so that Catholic children can get an adequate education and the laity can receive the services of the Church."

While Catholics in the United States have increased some 39 per cent in the last ten years the total number of priests, brothers, and sisters has risen only 18 per cent. Out of 3,000 counties in the United States, more than 1,000, or 30 per cent, are without resident priests.

Can laymen do anything to inspire new vocations for the Church? One group of Catholic men is showing that the laity *can* help. Known as Serra International, this organization of Catholic business and professional men has, for over twenty-five years, been laboring with singular resolve and untiring, often unsung, dedication to foster vocations. Because the members of Serra prefer to work in anonymity and avoid seeking personal glory or special publicity for themselves, this organization is still little known, but its accomplishments have made it one of the most remarkable lay movements in the modern history of the Church.

Serra began simply enough in the year 1934 with four Seattle, Washington, businessmen who got together for luncheon whenever they could. These Catholic men were deeply concerned about their Church and it was therefore natural that their luncheon discussions would usually move into the area of how they could fortify and encourage themselves in the practice of their faith, and how they could take a more active role in furthering the progress of the Church.

Other Catholic businessmen soon joined this foursome at their luncheons and before long these informal and friendly get-togethers had evolved into a definite organization. The men chose "Serra" as their name, in honor of Father Junipero Serra, the famous Franciscan missionary who founded the first missions in California. The purposes of the new group would be twofold: to foster priestly vocations and to assist in the education of young men for the priesthood. His Excellency the Most Reverend Gerald Shaughnessy, then Bishop of the Diocese of Seattle, suggested to the men that it would be a good idea to expand their organization beyond their own city. Taking the Bishop's good advice the first Serrans began to seek new members in other communities.

By 1938 Serra clubs had been established in Tacoma and Spokane, Washington, in Portland, Oregon, and in San Francisco. On July 2 of that year the established Serra clubs met in Seattle for their first convention and formed what is now known as Serra International.

It was an early supporter of this unique movement, Samuel Cardinal Stritch, who first set forth the way he believed Serra should be run if it was to accomplish fully the high purposes it had set for itself. "Let each club keep itself a small club," the Cardinal suggested. "Serra shouldn't be a mass organization. Each Serra Club must be a group of carefully selected and select Catholic men . . . we should have no deadwood in Serra Clubs. If members for one reason or another become inactive, they should be dropped from the roster of Serra Clubs."

The late Cardinal's unwavering advice became Serra's guiding principle.

The Catholic business and professional men who comprise Serra's membership are the select and dedicated laymen the good Cardinal had called for. At great personal sacrifice to themselves and their families, these men devote many hours away from their regular business and personal activities to help fulfill Serra's purposes. Each member is active, without exception. Each Serra Club is under a strict obligation to hold at least twenty-four meetings a year. Each Serran strives, of course, to attend every meeting but if he fails to attend at least 55 per cent of them he is dropped from the membership. Serrans themselves bring new members into the organization. When they find someone who they feel would make a good Serra member, they sponsor that person's membership without the candidate's knowing about it. This is done so as not to embarrass the man if for any reason he cannot join Serra. He has to be approved by his pastor and also stand up under a thorough investigation of his character and family life.

This rigid policy is, of course, not aimed at frightening any

Serran and priest preparing to show a vocations film to a group of Boy Scouts.

Catholics away from the movement, but rather to ensure that only those Catholic men with genuine loyalty to the organization's purpose of fostering vocations by deeds, not just by talk, will wish to become Serrans. The policy also serves to keep all Serra members constantly on their toes.

One Serran, who was also the president of a thriving business in a medium-sized Midwestern city, realized that after four years of devoted service to the organization, he had suddenly started to slacken his activities in the club. He was passing up more and more Serra luncheon meetings. He observed further that he wasn't the only member who had become delinquent in his meeting attendance. "I made up my mind to do something about it," the executive now recalls. "The first and third Mondays of every month are Serra days and I realized that I must be there. I made sure that all my business associates knew this too and didn't therefore invite me to luncheon on those days and thus tempt me to break my obligation to Serra."

Because of his improved attendance and renewed zeal for the movement the man was elected president of his club. He then went swiftly into action to reshape his entire club in the true Serra image. One third of the club's members had poor attendance records, he discovered. Acting with the approval of his club's board of trustees, the new president dispatched forceful letters to these eighteen members, informing them that because of their nonattendance at meetings it was considered that they had resigned from the club. They could, however, request reinstatement if they wished to do so. "Some of these men were personal friends of mine," the businessman recalls. "But I had promised myself not to let that factor enter into my thinking about this problem. I knew this was the only way to make our club stronger and more effective in fulfilling the purposes of the movement."

Thus, one Serran's devotion to his ideals started the needed chain reaction of dedication among the other members of his club. Attendance at meetings soared to 85 per cent; 3 per cent of the members who had been dropped asked for and received reinstatement, and the club became a group of 100 per cent "doers"—all active workers for the cause of fostering vocations.

In this way Serra has grown to a worldwide membership of more than 10,000 "working" members. There are some 285 clubs in 16 countries. Pruning, weeding out the inactive, is a continuous process that the organization unswervingly follows, keeping faith with the late Cardinal Stritch's tenet: "Let Serrans be as they should be—or let them not be."

What is a typical Serran like? He is probably a man very much like George H. Smith. A gently smiling, white-haired family man in his early sixties, George Smith is a busy executive at a large company in Newark, New Jersey, who also devotes many hours, both day and night, to Serra work, and who has consistently been doing so since the first day he joined the movement in 1954. In addition to this, he also serves as an acolyte every Friday at the noon mass at St. Patrick's Pro-Cathedral in Newark. A former Serra president, Smith believes fervently that "never since the time of the Apostles have laymen had a greater opportunity to work with the clergy of all ranks than is their opportunity today." Mr. Smith further believes that such cooperation can be especially effective in the sphere of fostering vocations.

Often, while lecturing to a group of parents on why he feels they should consider vocations for their children, a parent will say to him, "You'd feel differently if it were your own child you were losing." To which Smith calmly replies, "My son Dick is a priest and my daughter Dorothy is a Dominican nun. And I'm able to visit with them more often than with my son Robert, who's a doctor, or my daughter Cynthia, who's a secretary. My children in the religious life live on the East Coast, whereas my other children live in California."

Smith points out that a large percentage of Serrans have

someone in their family in a religious order, and indeed there have been Serrans who have themselves become priests. Smith believes strongly that parents owe it to their children to take the lead in stressing to them the beautiful life of a priest, sister, or brother.

"My wife Mary and I always gave 'equal time' to vocations in our home," Smith told me. "When the children were younger it was the practice in our household for all of us to get together after the evening meal to discuss events of the day. During these discussions all sorts of ideas were put forth about occupations and professions to help the children in choosing their life's work. One such discussion centered around the great opportunity doctors and priests have to accomplish important and useful work for humanity. We placed no objections or obstacles in the way of our children's consideration of a religious life, and therefore we were not startled when two of them decided to enter religious orders and when one son chose the profession of medicine for his career."

"This is the great purpose of Serra," Smith continues, "to create a more favorable atmosphere in which vocations can flourish."

Serrans believe that every boy or girl who indicates an interest in the religious life should be encouraged to test his or her vocation in a seminary or novitiate without any fear of a stigma being attached to them should they later decide that they don't want to continue in the religious life. "There are now more than half a million Catholic men and women who have spent some time in a seminary or convent," Smith points out. "They should be commended for their courage in trying the religious life, and are to be admired rather than pitied."

To stimulate greater interest in vocations among the laity, Serrans have launched more than seventy-five different activities. Serra Clubs have set up vocation book racks in prominent places; a club in Los Angeles started its own loan fund for seminarians and a Pittsburgh club sponsors the advanced education of a priest in Rome. Some sixteen clubs have programs to find summer employment for seminary students, and Serra clubs maintain speakers' bureaus on vocations and show specially made vocation films at parochial schools and before church groups.

A vocations exhibit held a short while ago by a Serra Club in St. Louis, Missouri, drew some 96,000 visitors, many of them students from local and nearby Catholic schools.

Over four million vocation prayer cards and half a million vocation pamphlets were distributed in one recent year by Serran Clubs throughout the country. Clubs take altar boys interested in vocations on visits to seminaries and on special combination picnics and retreats. They also conduct essay contests on vocations. One such contest held recently drew a staggering 225,000 entries from boys and girls.

Vocation workshops for altar boys are an important activity of a number of Serra Clubs. In this congenial and informal atmosphere Church representatives speak to boys interested in the religious life and answer any questions they may have on vocations. The entire range of duties and obligations in a religious order are described to the boys, who listen with rapt attention. As George Smith explains, "If the boy seems to possess those admirable qualities that characterize a priest Serrans believe they should be told so. Who knows but that this may be just the thing to spark their imagination, and to create or firm up a desire to seriously consider a religious vocation? If the response from the youngster is encouraging, then they might well be advised to consider a religious vocation. With God working in His wondrous ways, the final decision would of course rest with the young person, his family, and his priest."

In their exalting work of fostering vocations, Serrans make full use of that most important aid—prayer. Every Serra meeting opens and closes with a prayer for vocations. Serra also sponsors a perpetual novena for vocations. During a recent eighteen-month period Serrans and their families offered an estimated one million Masses and Communions for vocations, and every day Serra's ten-thousand members pray for vocations.

Serra emphasizes that "only God can make a vocation," and the organization therefore modestly avoids taking credit for any actual vocations that may result from any of their varied activities. Yet it does happen that a Serran visiting a seminary will be told by several of the young seminarians there that they first became interested in the religious life while viewing a Serra film on vocations in their seventh- or eighth-grade classroom. Bishops and vocational directors have observed that the interest in vocations rises considerably following the conclusion of some Serra program in their area. In Liverpool, England, a short while ago, a Serra program brought in a record number of applications for the priesthood from young men in that city.

As Serra International passes its first quarter-century of service to holy Mother Church, its members can look back on the organization's very substantial accomplishments. And they can look forward as well to a future of continual growth and achievement, for, as the late Cardinal Stritch declared, "God has blessed this work and He will continue to bless this work."

# XXII

# Frank Smith — Racket Buster

EACH SUNDAY, Frank Smith, his wife Terry, and their five children can be seen in their regular pew at St. Theresa's Church in Sunnyside, Queens, New York. On the other days of the week Frank is still on the job serving his church and his community as an Assistant District Attorney and a courageous racket buster.

Forty-two-year old Frank Smith is small in stature, with close-cropped blond hair and boyish good looks. When he was a kid he wanted to play on the neighborhood baseball team, but he was always turned down by the other boys as being too short. So he had to settle for being mascot.

Back in September, 1942, Frank, then nineteen, decided he wanted to be a Marine and this time he wasn't going to be turned down. One year later, at Quantico, Virginia, he was commissioned a lieutenant, which soon brought him to Okinawa, where the Marines were fighting against tough, entrenched enemy forces. For a month Frank was only assigned odd jobs in the adjutant's office, while a short distance away the Battle of Sugar Loaf Hill raged on. The Japanese were hidden in caves and trenches on the reverse slope of the hill.

Whenever a Marine assault unit reached the summit of the hill the Japs would immediately pour out of their hiding places and heave a barrage of hand grenades into the Marines, forcing them to fall back with heavy losses.

Ten attempts had been made to get over Sugar Loaf, but every try had failed. The losses to the Marines were especially acute in the officer ranks, yet final victory on Okinawa probably depended on the taking of that red clay mound of hell.

It was early morning, cold and windy. Lieutenant Colonel William G. Robb entered the adjutant's office. "Tell your platoon to take it," he said to Frank, who, because of the heavy officer casualties, was now next in rank for the job. Frank assembled his men. He was to lead two platoons up and he had a plan that he hoped would finally stop the Japs.

The men reached the summit, just as the others had done, and the Japs were ready, but so was Frank. "Make a line along the crest of the hill," he shouted to his men. The Marines were strung like a tight wire across the slope. Frank took the most exposed position so that he could direct the action. Each of his men was stocked up with a good supply of hand grenades. Frank was going to hit the enemy with its own maneuver, but he was going to do it first. "Let 'em have it!" he yelled, and his men drew their hand grenades, yanked the pins, and heaved their salvos at the caves and foxholes of the enemy just as they were starting to come out. The morning calm was suddenly shattered as the grenades exploded with a loud roar, churning up the ground and blasting to pieces the enemy strongholds. As the grenade barrage continued Frank directed some of his other men to set up machine guns along the slope. "Keep up the fire," he shouted to the machine gunners as they sprayed the enemy with bullets. The Japs that survived the onslaught were now crawling out of their caves, stunned and bewildered by the attack. Frank had been wounded in the

*Jack Landess Co., Inc.*

Frank Smith

head and hand by some stray shrapnel but he continued to hold his position and to direct the battle.

Marine tanks were now moving around both flanks of the hill to join Frank and his men. They arrived for the mopping-up action. The enemy fire subsided. Frank was still on top of the hill. "Let's move down and clean this thing up," he called out as he waved his men forward.

At 1:00 P.M., May 18, 1945, Lieutenant Colonel Robb declared Sugar Loaf Hill secure, and young Frank Smith emerged from his first engagement with the enemy as the hero of the day.

The Marines moved on deeper into the island where the Japs were dug in behind other strongholds. On June 1 a battle raged for one of the enemy fortifications and Frank was leading his men in another assault up a steep cliff. Suddenly a sniper's bullet struck him in the stomach, hitting with such power that he was knocked backward and tumbled into a gulley. Corporal George Sladkiewicz saw Frank fall. Enemy fire crackled all around them but George, crawling on his belly, managed to reach Frank. He pulled the half-conscious and seriously wounded Marine out of the gulley and got him back to the rear.

Frank was stretched out on the sandy, battle-scarred beach. The heavy enemy fire was preventing the evacuation of the wounded to a hospital ship nearby. Medical corpsman John Perry, a big guy with a friendly smile, was working over Frank, doing all he could. "Bet you a dime I don't make it," Frank murmured painfully. Perry leaned close to him. "It's a bet," he said.

Finally the wounded were taken to the ship and Frank was immediately operated on. In a few days he was on his way to recovery. He looked around for Perry—after all, he owed him some dough—but he couldn't find him and a short while later he was returned to the States.

Frank Smith, the little guy who couldn't make the sandlot baseball team, was now a national hero. They said his taking of Sugar Loaf Hill was the toughest assignment ever given to an inexperienced officer. They gave him the Silver Star, the Purple Heart, a Presidential Citation, and the American Legion Silver Star, and when he was discharged in October, 1945, it was all crowned with a huge welcome home block party in his old neighborhood. Everybody turned out to give their hero a rip-roaring reception. As the crowd of neighborhood folks gathered around him Frank noticed one in particular, his childhood sweetheart, Terry Lenehan, now grown into a beautiful, dark-haired young woman. "That's the girl for me," Frank said right then and there. A year later they were married and Frank set about becoming a lawyer.

At night he went to Fordham Law School in New York and by day he worked as a union organizer, following in the footsteps of his dad, who was a prominent figure in local union and political activities.

Early in October, 1950, Frank had a date at the hospital. His second child had just been born, a daughter—Donna Jean they named her. "I've got good news too," Frank said as he brought his wife and their new addition out of the hospital. He drew a little piece of paper from his jacket pocket and unfolded it carefully. "It's my degree from Fordham, honey. All four of us are now going home," he smiled as they entered their car parked at the hospital curb.

Two years later Frank, now an up-and-coming lawyer in his community, received an appointment as an investigator in the District Attorney's office and was soon advanced to the post of Assistant District Attorney, with frauds and rackets as his special beat.

One of his first assignments involved fast-talking car salesmen who were "clipping" scores of servicemen as they came into New York on their way back from overseas duty. Complaints from some of the swindled GI's reached the DA's office and Frank took on the job of breaking the racket. He donned some rather nondescript clothes, so he wouldn't be too noticeable, and went down to the airport. A big skyliner was just taxiing in. Frank stood over by the side of the exitway and watched as a cluster of servicemen disembarked from the plane and anxiously made their way into the lobby. Then Frank saw a broadly smiling, well-dressed man walk up with swift strides to one of the servicemen. "Hey, pal, I've got a great deal for you on a brand new car," the man said as he buttonholed the GI. The place was swarming with such salesmen, all of them scampering about the airport, grabbing servicemen and practically pushing them into waiting cars where they'd be taken to side-street hotels. Here they'd be privately plied with sugary sales talks and finally suckered into buying cars that would later turn out to be used, beat-up, or overpriced. Frank had seen enough. He checked further and found that the salesmen didn't represent any reputable car dealer. It was time to move against these racketeers.

The next day another planeload of GI's arrived at the airport and, as usual, the salesmen were there waiting for them, but they had company this time. Frank and his associates in the rackets bureau were also there, armed with subpoenas. "Here's a little present for you," Frank said as he moved up beside one of the salesmen, who was just about to start his big spiel to an unwary serviceman. "You're wanted in the DA's office for a little statement," Frank intoned, while his associates passed out subpoenas to the other salesmen before they could cheat any more servicemen.

The evidence that Frank and his staff amassed was turned over to the military authorities, who moved fast to stop the racket dead. Warnings were sent to all servicemen, and the local authorities imposed a ban on the salesmen at the airport and at other places throughout the country where servicemen

Frank Smith (right) with President Kennedy and Adlai
E. Stevenson at New York's La Guardia Airport, January 19, 1962.

were known to congregate. "The car rackets are now non-existent," Frank told me with a great deal of pride.

Another time Frank's boyish appearance helped him break a racket. It was found that a record store in his community was selling smutty recordings to teen-agers. Frank dressed himself in a sharp sports jacket, colorful shirt, and pegged pants and sauntered into the suspected store. He went through the motions of looking through the record stacks for a few minutes. Then he moved up to the counter, behind which a pudgy salesman was standing. "Do you have any good party records? You know the kind I mean," Frank said in a humorous voice. "Sure, I know what you want," the salesman quickly replied as he pulled some jacketed records out from under the counter. Frank examined them carefully—it was what he wanted all right. "I'll take them," he said as he drew some dollar bills from his pocket. Then, just as the salesman was completing the sale, Frank leaned over the counter and announced, "I'm from the DA's office. You're under arrest."

A couple of teen-age boys were brought into Frank's office one afternoon. A policeman had spotted them target-shooting in their backyard with real guns and bullets. "We found the guns," the boys insisted in an annoyed tone as Frank questioned them, but Frank scented something bigger here. He had the guns checked through. One of his associates came back with a report: "These guns were part of a shipment of armaments stolen a few months ago on an East Side pier. The other guns and ammunition in that shipment have been turning up all over the city."

Carrying a search warrant, Frank went to the home of the boys and searched it thoroughly. In the basement, hidden behind some boxes, he found a veritable arsenal of guns and ammunition. The boys were brought in again for further questioning.

Confronted by Frank's new evidence the boys broke down.

"We bought the stuff from some guy who came around the neighborhood," they admitted. "He said he could supply anything, from machine guns on down." They gave Frank the address where they'd picked up the stuff. A vicious gang of hoodlums, calling themselves "Arsenals Inc.," was at work in the city. The alarm went out and the police, working on Frank's evidence, moved in. One gang member's arrest led to another until the ringleaders were cornered and captured and the whole mob clapped into jail. Frank's hunch had started the chain reaction of the law that broke "Arsenals Inc."

As a family man and a leading citizen of his community, Frank has always been deeply concerned about juvenile delinquency and its prevention. So when a few years ago Vincent Quinn, then District Attorney, got an idea for a new and unusual approach to the juvenile delinquency problem it was natural that he would want to give Frank a top role in it.

"We'll call it Operation Checkmate," he told Frank with great enthusiasm. "It'll be something quite different, something never really tried before. We'll go directly to the teenagers and discuss their problems with them. We'll ask them for their complaints, their ideas, anything they want to tell us. We'll let them hear straight from young people who have gotten into trouble with the law just why what they did was wrong and why these teen-agers shouldn't make the same mistakes. Above all we'll *listen* to the kids so they'll listen to us. Everything will be voluntary and completely aboveboard. What do you think, Frank?"

"It sounds great," Frank replied heartily. "When do we start?"

They started a week later at a Queens high school. The place was jam-packed with teen-agers, and they pulled no punches with their questions and comments. "Why don't we have more recreation places?" several youngsters asked. "Why do the police always chase us when we're just standing on a street corner not bothering anybody?" Frank quickly answered, "We'll look into these matters right away." This was no runaround; the matters were looked into and where corrections were necessary they were made. In this way Frank soon gained the confidence and respect of the young people. Instead of taking out their grievances, real and imagined, in the form of mischief or worse they were now bringing them straight to the men of the law and being listened to sympathetically.

"Operation Checkmate" is now going full-blast in Queens, and other communities in various parts of the country have modeled their own J D programs along the same lines. Queens today has the lowest rate of juvenile crime in the entire city of New York.

For Marine hero Frank Smith, now head of the Queens racket bureau, it all adds up to a rugged, eighteen-hour-a-day schedule. In the daytime Frank's out chasing loan sharks, mortgage swindlers, charity racketeers, and pornography purveyors. "I figure we conduct seven or eight investigations a week," Frank told me. At night he's still going, keeping up his successful law practice and speaking before civic groups, parent-teacher assemblies, and religious and fraternal organizations, meeting with the people of his community to warn them about frauds and rackets and to enlist their aid in the never-ending fight against crime.

One year Frank was chosen as Queens Man of the Year by the local Junior Chamber of Commerce, and a dinner was held in his honor. In the midst of the festivities Frank looked up from his place at the table and saw someone approaching who looked vaguely familiar. The man came closer. "How are you, Frank?" he said as he reached his hand across the table to clasp Frank's. "Well, I'll be——" Frank said with a grin of final recognition. "John Perry—the guy who was with me on the beach before I was taken out to the ship to be operated on!" "That's right," Perry said with a full smile. "I'm here to collect the dime you owe me."

# XXIII

# Centers for the Salvage
# of Human Beings

THE PLEASANT-LOOKING middle-aged woman stopped her automobile before the unpretentious-looking store-front. As she climbed out of her car she looked up and read the words emblazoned on the sign over the store's door, words that set this simple place apart from the others lining the street: SALVAGE BUREAU OF THE ST. VINCENT DE PAUL SOCIETY.

The woman entered. Within the store there was a beehive of activity. Men and women were intently and busily examining the wares on the shelves and tables—picture frames, lamps, clothing of all kinds, furniture and bric-a-brac. Even several good-toned organs stood against a back wall. All these goods had been donated by the people of the city to help the less fortunate among them.

"I have something to give," the woman announced in a strong, determined voice to one of the store's staff. "At Mass the father made an appeal for the Salvage Bureaus and I want to give my automobile."

The people of the Salvage Bureaus have learned to take even the most staggering donation in stride. "The important thing now," one staff member said, "is to find someone who urgently needs this woman's generous gift."

A few weeks later the need was located. A nearby hospital for convalescents was using a station wagon to ferry its out patients back and forth from the hospital. The Salvage Bureau's staff knew that the hospital could put another car to very good use and that they didn't have the funds to purchase one. So a few days later the hospital was the car's proud owner, without any cost to them.

For over fifty years the Salvage Bureaus have been engaged in this great task of "bearing witness to Christ and his Church by working for the good of humanity." The Bureaus are operated quietly, without fanfare, their staff members and volunteer helpers preferring to remain anonymous, letting their good deeds of Christian charity speak for them.

The first recorded opening of a Bureau was in Philadelphia in the year 1911. The Bureau idea was conceived as a means of fulfilling the desire of the founder of the Society of Saint Vincent de Paul, Antoine Frédéric Ozanam (1813–1853), that Society members deepen their own faith through spiritual and corporal works of mercy. The Bureaus, it was decided, would procure usable goods for the poor by salvage rather than purchase.

"The early days of this venture were filled with trials and tribulations," states the Reverend Daniel T. McColgan in describing the Philadelphia store in his history of the Society, *A Century of Charity.*

"There were some who felt that it exercised a degrading influence upon the beneficiaries. However, the protagonists pushed the matter forward, and with the cooperation of the Archbishop, the parish clergy, and people, a small storehouse was rented and a few teams hired. Then followed a campaign of informal parochial advertising, with laudable results. The public responded wholeheartedly and generously, insuring the unfaltering forward progress of the work."

Today there are more than two hundred "salvage stores"

dotting the country, employing more than two thousand people and backed by volunteer Vincentians, who give freely of their time and energy to help others.

Here is how a typical Salvage Bureau in one of our large cities operates:

One afternoon the telephone rang in the office of the store's director. The call was from the Mother Superior of a home for the aged. She had phoned to thank the Bureau for sending the home some much-needed medical supplies, and also because she had an unusual request to make.

"Would it be possible for you to find a fiddle for one of our residents? It would certainly give him a new lease on life." The man had been a musician when he was younger, the Mother Superior explained, and now, with his family gone, he could only think about his music and how much it meant to his peace of mind.

There were no violins in the store, the director discovered, so the store's staff went to work trying to find one. They asked everyone they knew if they could put them in touch with someone who would like to donate a violin in good working order to a man whose need for it was so vital and purposeful. After several weeks of searching they found their donor, himself a professional musician. "I'm sure this violin will be of greater use in the hands of this man than in mine. Please take it," the man said in selfless charity.

It was a heartwarming event when the violin was presented as a gift to the elderly man at the home. He fingered the instrument gently and held it close. His strong, lined face shone with excitement and his eyes brightened as he lifted the bow and began to play. The man's life was now enriched and useful once again. Now he would have many moments of joy as he played and his music would also bring great pleasure to the other residents of the home.

At another time an official of a local parish school called to ask if the store had a piano as the school did not have the funds to purchase one.

Today the school has a good-toned piano, its donor unknown, the instrument itself of immeasureable aid to the students and teachers at the school in their music lessons.

One day a young dentist came into the salvage store and said to a staff member, "I'm refurnishing my office with completely new equipment. I have all my old equipment, which still has plenty of good use in it. You can have all of it. Perhaps you can find someone who can put it to use to help others."

The store's staff inquired around to find a good use for the equipment. From a local cancer hospital they received word that they could indeed use such equipment. "It will enable us to concentrate our efforts on the care of the sick poor," an official of the hospital said. Today the hospital has its own dental clinic serving the community, due to the salvage principle in action.

One afternoon a priest called to tell about the great need of one of his parishioners. She was an elderly woman who had very faulty vision. Her income was tiny and she couldn't work because of her vision problem. If there were only a lamp available for her, the father suggested, the woman would be able to read and this would give her daily life a great lift.

The store's staff not only found the woman a lamp, but they located one equipped with an extra-bright bulb designed especially for those with faulty vision.

Salvage stores like this one aren't run to make a profit. They exist to help people help others, not actually to sell goods. The most important thing is getting the donated materials where they will do the most good. A short while ago this store took a load of donated books and magazines to a nearby center for homeless men to add to the center's library of good reading material.

There is one aspect, however, of the store's work that does include the selling of goods, but this is also done in a charitable manner. People of limited means come to the store to purchase goods that they badly need but can't afford to buy at the regular stores. These people gladly pay a nominal cost for these goods. By so doing they preserve for themselves a sense of self-dignity, self-responsibility, and independence. By paying for the goods as best they can they feel that nobody is giving them something for nothing. (Some Salvage Bureaus, in fact, have work-in-exchange-for-commodity arrangements by which those unable to pay cash for the goods they want can work instead at the salvage stores, thereby earning the amount needed for their purchase.)

The people who buy at the salvage stores, while not well-blessed with the world's goods, are still cheerful, happy, and alert to finding the goods they like and can afford. All the money realized from these sales goes to support the various charitable activities of the Society.

This salvage store also helps in the resettlement of needy families. In this important facet of its work the Bureau works closely with local social agencies.

A short while ago a destitute family was finally able to move out of its overcrowded furnished room into larger but unfurnished quarters. But now they faced the prospect of being plagued by a debt for furniture that would have to be met week by week out of the family's meager earnings. The Bureau was apprised of the situation by the social agency handling the case and asked to help if they could.

A few days later, a moving van came to a stop before the apartment house into which the family had moved and delivered to them a full set of furniture and other needed goods to furnish the entire apartment. It was all given without charge to start the family out debt-free and with renewed hope for the future.

In another instance, a young woman had just arrived in town from her native Virgin Islands. She could only speak French and she had little money, two serious problems for a stranger in a large, bustling city. The Salvage Bureau heard of the woman's plight. Fortunately a staff member spoke both French and German so he was able to bridge the language obstacle for her. The woman then located an apartment for herself, but she had no money for furnishings. The salvage store again came to her rescue. She received a bed, lamps, blankets, and clothing. "This is certainly a very friendly city," the woman exclaimed as she gazed joyfully at the abundance of gifts provided for her by the charity of others.

Salvage Bureaus like this one and others throughout the country are supported by the Catholic and non-Catholic public, who generously contribute articles they can no longer use but which can still be used by the needy, sick, and helpless. A number of salvage stores even offer paid employment to handicapped and aged persons, and as Father McColgan points out further in his book, "The Bureaus have contributed large shipments of clothing to deserving groups . . . abroad. From this depot, supplies of good Catholic literature have been made available for distribution by the Vincentian visitors in the city hospitals and almshouses. Many a destitute person has left an institution not only improved in mind but with some sartorial splendor, due to the Salvage Bureaus."

The salvage stores are not only places for material objects but also instruments for the promotion of the spiritual good of humanity. In Father McColgan's view these stores are "centers for the salvage of human beings."

# XXIV

# Courageous Convert-Makers

FATHER ERWIN A. JURASCHEK, a tall, husky priest, stood on the podium inside the Pontiac, Michigan, meeting place and looked out at the good-sized audience seated in front of him. He was holding his briefcase in his hand and without saying a word he reached into it and took out what everyone in the large room recognized as a doorbell. He held the object up and began to ring it loudly, much to the surprise and wonderment of the audience.

The Texas priest, it turned out, was just illustrating a point. "We need a doorbell apostolate," he exclaimed. "We need a convert for every Catholic layman in the United States. Give us that, and in twenty years all America would be Catholic— and soon the entire world under 'one fold and one Shepherd.'"

Father Juraschek uttered these words before an audience that he knew would be fully responsive to his challenge. All those present at this meeting were members of an unusual and highly effective Catholic lay organization, The Convert-Makers of America (CMOA). For over twenty years this group has devoted its energies to the great task of intelligently presenting the truth about Catholicism to those outside the Church.

CMOA was the offspring of the religious dedication of three people, a laywoman, a priest, and a seminarian. The laywoman was Margaret Lynch (now Mrs. Robert Gibson, and mother of five children). While a student in high school Margaret became acutely aware that all too many public school students harbored serious misconceptions about the Church. When she left high school she determined to do something to help inform non-Catholics of just what the Church really believes. She began what she proudly calls her "apostolate of vocalizing the Faith" by speaking to non-Catholic acquaintances, in pleasant and cordial tones, and telling them why their fears and apprehensions about the Catholic Church had no justification in fact. But she found that she was almost alone in this much-needed work. All too many other Catholics, she discovered, were reluctant to discuss the Church with non-Catholics, for they feared that they were not qualified for such a task and that they would therefore do more harm than good. "What is needed is organized methods by which Catholics can become effective convert-makers," Margaret decided.

In 1944 she enrolled for a course in convert-making at the Summer School of Catholic Action at San Antonio, Texas, sponsored by the Queen's Work of St. Louis, Missouri. The course was taught by Father John E. Odou, S.J., and one of the students in Margaret's class was Erwin Juraschek, then a seminarian.

Both Father Odou and the young seminarian had been thinking for some time about an effective way to create young adult convert-makers, precisely Margaret's idea. Thus, three people from different parts of the country had been providentially brought together to give life to the great idea they shared in common.

It happened near the end of the course. The three were talking about their idea when Erwin Juraschek suddenly made a chance suggestion. "Perhaps our class could form the nucleus of the convert-making organization," he said, and before they knew it CMOA was born.

Other laymen and laywomen joined the founding group and a set of guiding principles for the infant organization was developed. There would be no dues or regular meetings. Instead, the members would be linked to the organization through a unique program of reports and bulletins. Each member would have a priest advisor to whom he or she would send weekly reports telling him of their convert-making progress and asking any questions they might have on doctrine or procedures they could follow to strengthen their apostolate. The part played by the two religious founders of the organization would be vitally important. Father Odou and seminarian Juraschek would provide the theological correctness and the ecclesiastic line of command without which this effective Catholic Action would never have been possible.

The members integrated their activities into the work of already established Catholic organizations and parish groups. Most of all they went forth with courage and zeal, as the Apostles did, to bring the Faith to the multitudes. What had started as just The Convert-Makers of America now became the more forthright Convert-Making Our Apostolate.

By the end of its first year CMOA had over ninety members who had already successfully effected some twenty-four conversions.

In 1946 a Chicago man, Edward Ellinanger, gave CMOA the idea for a "pamphlet-rack apostolate" and from this the organization embarked on an ambitious program of placing information racks of free Catholic literature in railroad stations, bus depots, hotels, and other public places. This literature would expose the falsehoods being circulated about the Catholic Church. Today there are more than a thousand CMOA information racks set up at many points throughout the United States, including Alaska, and in Canada, from which thousands of pieces of free literature are distributed every week, making Catholic truths easily accessible to all who frequent these places.

In 1949 CMOA, backed by the contributions of well-wishers and the modest funds raised through the sale of its convert-making literature, established headquarters in rented space at 1093 Boston Avenue in Pontiac. The headquarters would be staffed by volunteers and one salaried clerical helper. The membership had by now climbed to more than three thousand, and CMOA members were winning many converts by talking to non-Catholics, by distributing literature, and often simply in those "mysterious ways" in which the Lord sometimes works. Like this incident:

Margaret had been corresponding with a friend and explaining to her just what the Church believes. But the woman was staunchly set in her own religious beliefs and, try as hard as she could, Margaret still couldn't quite get her to take the final steps to conversion. But the woman did pass along Margaret's letters and literature to some other members of her family. Several years later Margaret learned that, without her knowing it, her letters had influenced her friend's mother, sister, and nephew to embrace Catholicism.

Other CMOA members were also devoting considerable time and energy to their self-assigned mission for the Faith. A member in Harvey, Illinois, was distributing pamphlets on the Church through doctors' offices, at train and bus stations, and at filling stations. A New York member was circulating Catholic literature in hospitals and public places and never letting an opportunity go by to engage people in conversation about the Faith. A St. Louis member decided to specialize in convert-making among Armed Forces personnel. She began to distribute, personally and by mail, about six-hundred pieces of literature each week to servicemen and women. And, as their regular reports to their priest-advisors testified, they were all bringing new faithful into the Church.

A short while ago CMOA member Laura Aman, a gentle-faced, soft-voiced former schoolteacher, now in her sixties, pridefully announced that she had made her 262nd baptised convert.

How does one build up such a remarkable record? For Laura, who has always been deeply devoted to the Church, such a feat came naturally. It started in 1949 with Laura's retirement from her job in the federal government. That year she began what she now calls "the happiest and most rewarding years of my life."

One Sunday morning Laura was on a bus in Cincinnati, Ohio, on her way to a Holy Name Parade. An elderly Negro woman surrounded by six young Negro children was seated near her. Laura moved closer to the woman and began to talk to her. The woman identified herself as Mrs. Boyd. She told Laura that the children were all members of her Sunday school and that she was now taking them to visit some Catholics and learn about their faith.

"I'm a former schoolteacher," Laura told the woman. "If you wish, I'll be glad to come to your Sunday school and answer any questions you and your children have about the Catholic Church."

Laura is white and her offer especially impressed the Negro woman. "That will be wonderful," she said. "The fact that you are willing to give your time to teach us colored people shows how free you are from prejudice and how eager you are to share your spiritual treasure with us."

The Sunday school turned out to be just one room in a run-down, unpainted building. But here Mrs. Boyd and her children were sincerely searching for the way they could best serve God, though they were not at that time actually affiliated with any specific religious group. Laura sat before the class one Sunday morning and graciously answered their questions.

"Was the Catholic Church founded by Christ for colored

people as well as for the whites?" one small-faced Negro youngster asked her.

"Yes, the Catholic Church is the church of all peoples, tribes,
and nations," Laura replied. "Like her Divine founder, she is
no respecter of persons, no discriminator against people because
of shades of complexion. She loves the colored people and
welcomes them not only into her churches but also into her
schools, seminaries, convents, and monasteries."

After she had answered their questions and told them about
the Church Laura invited Mrs. Boyd and the children to attend
Sunday Mass with her. Laura also started giving instructions to
Mrs. Boyd's family and some of her friends, and she began to
teach the catechism to the ten- to fourteen-year-old youngsters
in the class.

A short while later Mrs. Boyd became a Catholic, as did a
number of the Sunday school children. In addition, Laura's
efforts bore fruit in the neighborhood where Mrs. Boyd lived,
for several of her friends also joined the Church.

After that, Laura became a full-time convert-maker. She
began to give instructions in a county home for the aged and at
the General Hospital of Cincinnati. She also started an instruction class at her parish, the Holy Trinity Church, and even
began to teach elderly and disabled people in their own homes.
Later she had the great satisfaction of seeing a number of these
shut-ins baptized in their homes.

"In this work of convert-making, the biggest factor is the
grace of God given to the prospective convert, and that person's
free cooperation and willingness to investigate and listen to
Catholic teaching," Laura told me. "I use a logical and clear
presentation I start to speak about my subject at first and then
attempt to bring God into the conversation. Most people believe
in God and they will usually say something about Him at this
point. We should listen, and by their comments we will know
how to proceed and how to appeal to them.

"Later I say that as long as we wish to learn about God, we should learn from the greatest teacher of all, His Son, Jesus. I often explain that Jesus wanted all mankind to learn correctly about God. For that purpose He spent three years teaching people, especially His Twelve Apostles. He knew that He was to be crucified and buried, that He would rise again. He remained on earth for forty days after His resurrection on Easter Sunday for two reasons: to let people see Him and talk with Him and therefore be able to say with certainty that He surely did rise from the dead, and also to finish the instruction of the Apostles and to found His one Church, which would continue to teach mankind until the end of time."

Recently Laura suffered a serious heart attack and had to stop her convert-making activities, at least temporarily. "When my doctor allows me to go out again I must not be as active as I was before but I am going to do as much as possible," Laura says with the same firm resolution that has characterized all her "happy years" of service to the Church.

The dedication of "convert-makers" like Laura Amans is matched by the zeal and diligence of CMOA's volunteer helpers, who give their time freely at the organization's new headquarters at 268 West Pike Street in Pontiac, attending to the thousand and one small but important details that buttress and often actually make possible the accomplishments of the actual convert-makers. One such volunteer worker is a gray-haired woman in her early sixties, Mrs. Gertrude Anderson. Herself a convert to Catholicism, Gertrude decided to put her extensive educational background to work for the cause. Therefore, in St. Benedict's Church in Pontiac Mrs. Anderson knelt by the altar and pledged a year of her time as a "doer" for CMOA, a promise she has faithfully kept.

Today, CMOA's membership encompasses forty-nine states and the Philippine Islands. Approximately five-thousand people have already been trained by the organization and there are about one-hundred new trainees every year, plus thousands more who are reached through lectures and summer-school courses. To make every Catholic an effective messenger of the Faith is CMOA's goal, for as Laura Amans confided to me, "If only other Catholics would realize the joy and rewards here on earth for bringing people to the Church they would go out and make converts too."

# XXV

# Dick Rendich's Modern Crusade

"THE OPPORTUNITIES for family Communion are greater now than ever before. Children can now receive Communion earlier, and the practice itself is today much more widely accepted than it was in past years."

This is the view of Henry Mannix, a New York attorney and Catholic lay leader, who has been practicing the family Communion idea with his own loved ones for some thirty-five years.

Henry and Mary Margaret Mannix have nine children. "As soon as the children were old enough, we began to gather at the altar rail together each week," Mannix, a moderately tall, gray-haired man, said recently. "This had a wonderful effect in our family by serving as a good example for our children. We know that the children have led a better life because we followed this practice. We have always made the practice voluntary for our children, not compulsory. In this way we feel that the children go to family Communion only when they want to. It is up to parents to create a desire in their children to want to receive the sacrament with them. Parents, of course, should make clear to their children the essential conditions for a worthy reception of Holy Communion."

Four of the Mannix children are now married, and Henry and his wife are the proud grandparents of twenty-eight grandchildren. "Our married children are now following the family Communion idea as frequently as possible, and several grandchildren are now old enough to go to Communion," Henry Mannix says proudly.

Henry and his wife haven't confined the good effect of their family Communion practice to their own family circle. They have also been instrumental in encouraging others outside their family to achieve the blessings that flow from this very special form of devotion.

The Mannix family regularly attends St. Francis of Assisi Church near their home in Mount Kisco, New York. When they first started to gather together at the altar rail of the church a few years ago, shortly after moving into the vicinity, they were almost alone in their practice of this devotion. But soon other members of the parish began to notice the Mannix family and to perceive the deep joyousness they were gaining from their Communion together. Before long, other families in the parish were taking their place beside them at the altar rail. Today, the number of families receiving Communion together at the church has increased so greatly that the first Sunday of each month has been designated as "Family Communion Day" at St. Francis parish.

In view of Henry Mannix's dedication to the family Communion idea it is only logical that he should be on the Board of Directors and a past president of the Family Communion Crusade, an international organization of Catholic families dedicated to honoring the Holy Family through the regular reception of Holy Communion in family groups. The Crusade began as the personal and deeply felt apostolate of a devout man, Dr. Richard Rendich.

"Dick and I had been friends for many years," Henry Mannix points out. "Words are really inadequate to fully describe

The late Dick Rendich and his wife Claire.

The Donald Graham family of Wantagh, New York,
receive Holy Communion from Reverend Bernard Ryan.

this man. He was a gentle, saintly person, cheerful and fervent in everything he sought to accomplish."

One evening in 1950, Henry received a phone call from Dick. "He was very excited," Mannix remembers. "He told me he was starting a new and unique Catholic lay movement. It would be a crusade to promote the practice of family Communion all over the world. He asked me if I would like to join. I quickly told him that I thought his idea was wonderful and that indeed the Mannix family had been practicing family Communion for just about all of our married life, and that all of us believed in the idea very strongly."

"Dick didn't want any money from me or from anyone else to finance his new organization," Mannix says further. "He insisted on paying all the expenses out of his own pocket, as he didn't want people to think that they were under any burdensome financial obligation if they joined his movement. All he wanted was for people to believe in his idea and to do all they could to help spread the Crusade. He also said that he wanted the Crusade always to remain a lay movement, since it would be the layman who would benefit most by adopting the family Communion idea. Dick emphasized that the Crusade would not be an organization in the strict sense of the word, but rather would be a spiritual movement, so that any Catholic society, guild, or group could include the Crusade idea among their own activities."

This was the beginning of the Family Communion Crusade as a lay movement, but actually Dick Rendich's own personal crusade for family Communion had begun many years before.

Dick was born in Brooklyn, New York, on September 6, 1891, the fifth child in what would eventually be a family of ten children. The modest and always neatly kept Rendich home was a model of sacramental life. The Rendichs upheld their Christian principles with meticulous and loving care. "From my parents I learned to look on the Holy Eucharist as a binding agent that would provide a solid foundation for any family," Dick remarked some years later.

Starting his formal education, first at St. Stephen's School in Brooklyn and then at St. Francis School in New York City, Dick found himself drawn to the profession of medicine as a way in which he could best serve his fellow man. He attended Brooklyn Preparatory School and then Fordham University's Medical School.

While a student at the medical school, Dick began to attend the chapel at Fordham with several of his fellow students, and on the first Friday of each month they received Communion together.

One cold and rainy Friday in 1912, Dick witnessed an incident that was to have a profound effect on the course of his life. As he sat in the back of the chapel, he watched a family—father, mother, and three children, ranging in age from six to ten—walk up to the altar rail together. As the family walked back from the Communion rail, the young medical student observed the spiritual look of joy on each of their faces. "They now have Christ held close to their hearts," Dick thought to himself.

The young man was deeply affected by the incident, and a short while later he began to receive monthly Communion with his own family.

Upon graduating from Fordham, Dick went into the then new medical fields of roentgenology and radiology, and in a few years he was recognized as an authority in both fields. He was cofounder and president of the Catholic Physicians Guild in the Diocese of Brooklyn and president of the Federation of Catholic Physicians.

In 1927, Dick married the former Claire Jobin, to whom he had been introduced by a mutual friend. Though their marriage was never blessed with children, Dick and Claire continued to follow the family Communion practice with their own immediate families on the first Friday of each month. The example they set encouraged a number of other families to join them at the altar rail.

On January 8, 1950, on the Feast of the Holy Family, twenty-eight members of the Rendich family were seated together at a family Communion breakfast at St. Charles Borromeo Church in Brooklyn. A short while before, they had all received Holy Communion together. It was at this moment, with his family gathered happily around him, that Dick reflected to himself on the many graces he and his loved ones had received over the years since they had begun to practice family Communion. Dick decided that others should also have the opportunity to receive these benefits, and thus the idea for the Family Communion Crusade finally crystallized in his mind.

He hurriedly phoned his friends, among them Henry Mannix, and enlisted their moral support in his new, challenging apostolate. The response from his friends was so overwhelmingly enthusiastic that Dick appealed to the Most Reverend Archbishop-Bishop of Brooklyn, Thomas E. Molloy, for episcopal approval of his idea and official permission to promote family Communion as widely as possible. The approval came on June 15, 1950.

While keeping up his successful medical practice, Dick also managed to put in many hours each day promoting the Crusade. He set up working space in the basement of his Brooklyn home and, with Claire's complete support and help, started to build his Crusade, determined to make it a worldwide movement.

Dick's advisor from the start was Monsignor Paul Faustmann, of the Brooklyn diocese. Father Faustmann was a tireless and devoted worker for Dick's cause. He gathered volunteers to help, and he himself spent his days off working with Dick on the Crusade. And it was Father Faustmann who became the Crusade's spiritual moderator and a strong moving force in the growth of the idea. When the going got rough it was the enthusiasm and encouragement of these friends and of his wife that buoyed up Dick's courage and kept him going.

The founding group, Dick, Claire, Father Faustmann, and a handful of volunteer helpers, managed to turn out thousands of individually typed letters about the Crusade, which they sent to bishops and priests in many sections of the country and overseas, asking for their cooperation in spreading the word about the Crusade. A few thousand families joined the Crusade, but to Dick and his faithful followers this was but a mustard seed that must grow into an enormous tree.

It was while engaged in this dedicated activity that Dick was suddenly stricken with a heart attack. He decided, therefore, to retire from his medical practice.

To Dick the heart attack was "God's providence." Now he could devote all his time and energy to promoting the Crusade. He and his helpers put in many exhausting hours making up packages of leaflets to inform others about the Crusade, typing hundreds of letters, and planning campaigns. Dick spent thousands of dollars of his own money to keep the Crusade going.

The Rendichs lived comfortably, but never extravagantly. Rather than buy the Cadillac they could well have afforded, Dick and Claire preferred a Ford, putting the money saved into the Crusade.

One day in 1955, Dick had a special visitor in his home, Father Hector C. Lemieux, S.S.S. At that time the capable, gentle-voiced priest was the editor of the magazine published by the Blessed Sacrament Fathers. He had heard about the Crusade and was most anxious to learn more about it. It was this that brought him to Dick's home.

In the midst of their discussion of the Crusade, Dick suddenly sprang his newest idea on the attentively listening priest. "I don't know how much more time God has allotted me on earth," Dick said thoughtfully. "I want to make sure, though, that the Crusade continues even after I am gone, and I feel that the best way to do this would be for the Crusade to be taken under the wing of some religious order. Do you think the Blessed Sacrament Fathers would want to 'adopt' our movement? The direction of the Crusade would of course always remain in the hands of laymen, but the priests and brothers of the religious order would handle the detailed work of the direct mail campaign that is now the Crusade's main method for attracting new members."

Father Lemieux proposed Dick's idea to his superiors, and some time later Dick received the joyful news that the congregation had agreed to handle the paper work of the Crusade. A group of Blessed Sacrament Fathers was assigned to work full time for the movement at the order's novitiate, an imposing three-story brick building stretching across a large acreage of well-kept grounds in Barre, Massachusetts. A modern printing plant was erected at the novitiate and its facilities were also put at the movement's disposal.

Dick continued his own work for the Crusade, and when death finally came to him, in October, 1956, it was an easy death, attended by the knowledge that the good work he had started would prosper in the capable hands of the priests and laymen of the movement.

"Dick had left us all a great legacy, and we knew that we must continue his idea in the way he would have wanted," says Father Lemieux, now executive director of the Crusade.

The Crusade's campaign gets under way each summer, some six months before the Feast of the Holy Family, which is celebrated on the first Sunday after Epiphany. Although the Crusade is seeking to encourage family Communion as a regular once-a-month occasion, the Feast of the Holy Family has been chosen as the movement's rallying point. This day has been set aside as a time when all Catholic families are urged to receive

Communion as a unit and thus consecrate the entire family to the Holy Family.

Dick provided in his will for the continuing financial stability of the movement. After providing for his wife, and with her full and wholehearted approval, he left the rest of his estate to the Crusade.

The Crusade is a truly cooperative effort, with priests and laymen working side by side to carry its message to every possible point in the world.

During the campaign period, letters go out to every bishop of every diocese in the world, to heads of religious orders, and to individual priests in this country and overseas. The letters briefly explain the Crusade's purposes and offer to supply each recipient with leaflets (describing the Crusade and its objectives) that can be distributed to their parishioners. The leaflets are available free of charge in any quantity the recipient wishes and in any language. If the person wishes the leaflets in a language not already available, the Crusade has the leaflet translated into the language requested and a supply printed and mailed. During one recent year, more than six million leaflets were distributed, printed in eighty-one languages, from Chinese to English, from Amharic (a language of Ethiopia) to Paluan (a language of the Caroline and Marshall Islands) to Visayan (a language of the Philippines). In addition, some one-hundred-thousand posters telling of the Crusade were distributed.

About three-hundred-fifty radio stations across the country carry regular spot announcements of the Crusade during the six months' promotion period, and when the Feast of the Holy Family comes, an estimated one million families in the United States and other countries—Africa, India, Korea, and dozens more—spiritually link hands at the Communion rail, and come away with their family spirit and devotion to the Church greatly fortified.

The effects of the Crusade are everywhere to behold. In the small village of Goiás in the mountainous hill country of Brazil there had at one time been serious religious apathy among the village men. Many of them had come to believe that it was undignified for them to attend church. Then the Crusade leaflets came and were passed around from family to family. The men started to carry them in their pockets and read them over and over. Soon many decided to try the family Communion way. They returned to their village church with their families and soon they also began to participate in other church services. Before long that little village church was crowded to capacity with entire families of the faithful.

In other villages in Brazil, the same great upsurge of interest in the Church followed in the wake of the distribution of Crusade leaflets in each area, so much so that His Excellency Dom Emmanuel, Archbishop of Goiás, said to a priest in his village, "I hear the Family Communion Crusade is revolutionizing the families in your district." In another village in Brazil, seven more churches had to be built to minister to the great numbers of people flocking to church following the adoption of the Crusade.

In the United States the results have been equally phenomenal. One church increased its annual reception of Holy Communion from 12,000 to 43,000 after its members began to practice family Communion.

One day, a short while ago, the pastor of a church in Allston, Massachusetts, stood on the steps of his church and observed a joyful sight. His parishioners were coming down the street toward him, walking together in family groups. And inside the church the families sat together, prayed together, and came to the altar rail together.

A young girl in Massachusetts was so deeply inspired by the Crusade that she started a club in her area to get more families interested in the family Communion idea, and various religious clubs and diocesan councils have begun to incorporate the Crusade idea into their own programs.

Several churches in New York have found the idea so popular with their parishioners that they have made family Communion a weekly occasion.

"I know that Dick would have been greatly heartened to see how his Crusade has grown and spread, and to know that now millions are embracing the idea he so humbly but fervently advanced," Father Lemieux concludes. "And since Dick was convinced that family Communion could be a source of great spiritual and moral enrichment for families everywhere, I think he would have been especially gratified if he could have heard the words of a woman in Michigan who said, 'Never have I been happier than on the Sundays my husband and I knelt with our three sons at the altar rail.'"

## XXVI

# The Greatest
# Crusade of Its Kind

THE BEAUTIFUL words and music of the *Ave Maria* filled
the New York stadium as the 76,000 people gathered together
on that pleasantly warm October day in 1952 lifted their
voices in song. Here were people from all walks of life, joined
on this day by the bond of the Family Rosary, the inspiring
movement for world prayer inaugurated in Washington, D.C.,
by a humble, determined Irish priest, and now blossomed forth
into what has been often called "the greatest crusade of its
kind."

At the center of the stadium field there had been erected a
high platform shaped like a cross, which was surmounted by
an altar. The slogan of the Family Rosary Crusade, "The
Family That Prays Together Stays Together," had been placed
on a eighty-foot pylon, and near it was a twelve-foot statue of
the Virgin Mary.

This huge meeting, one of many that had been or were yet
to be held in cities throughout the world, was presided over by
Francis Cardinal Spellman, assisted by approximately one
hundred priests from nearby parishes. About a month before,
60,000 laymen from 387 New York parishes had personally

visited hundreds of homes asking people to sign the Rosary pledge, which stated simply: "To obtain peace for the nations of the world and the love and protection of God and Mary for myself and the members of my family, I pledge the daily Family Rosary." This giant meeting was thus the climax of that painstaking campaign, providing a chance for New Yorkers of all faiths, to pledge and sing together.

The Family Rosary Crusade was founded by Father Patrick Peyton, a young, courageous priest who was stirred to begin this monumental project by his earnest belief that "we need God in these days of stress and distress. We need him perhaps as never before, so urgent and so crucial are the crises that now beset us."

It was late in 1941 when Father Peyton first got the idea of starting the Family Rosary Crusade. He had just been ordained and was meditating solemnly in a chair on the lawn of Holy Cross College in Washington, D.C. He was thinking deeply, trying to decide to what purpose he should dedicate his priesthood, when he remembered back to his early years in Ireland, to the religious life that had been practiced there with methodical care, and the great happiness and family peace that the people of his village had derived from the Rosary prayers they'd said together each night. The families would gather at twilight, Father Peyton recalled, and recite the Rosary. That day Father Peyton pledged to God that he would bring the Rosary devotion to ten million homes, that he would travel about the world, speaking to everyone he could, kings and commoners, in an effort to bring family prayer back into every home. Through the subsequent years of struggle and sacrifice Father Peyton has clung with unyielding determination to that promise.

In the beginning, the going wasn't easy. After his graduation Father Peyton was sent to Albany, New York, to fill a chaplain's post and it was there in New York's capital city that the foundation for his Rosary Crusade was laid. It began with speeches made in small churches and schools throughout the city. "We must bring family prayer back into the home." Father Peyton's dynamic words rang through dozens of Albany halls and auditoriums, moving hundreds to respond to his call. Not content with just speeches, Father Peyton sat down at his desk one night and drew up a score of letters describing his plans, which he intended to send out to as many religious leaders as he could. He had no money for the postage, but the father soon discovered that the people he had spoken to about his crusade were sincere in their wish to help. Money came into Father Peyton's home in small but indeed welcome quantities. He would find coins and dollar bills tucked under his door, under his plate at dinner time, or in the mail. The responses to his hundreds of speeches and to the letters he was finally able to mail were coming in with encouraging speed, but he still felt that the great need and urgency of the Family Rosary Crusade warranted even speedier growth.

One day he visited the local radio station in Albany, WABY, and so moved and impressed the officers of the station with his idea that they granted him fifteen minutes of free time on their station. This one broadcast, which succeeded in bringing the message of the Family Rosary Crusade into thousands of homes, now has grown into the weekly half-hour program called "The Family Theatre," which has an estimated worldwide audience of over ninety million listeners.

When Father Peyton first approached some experienced radio men with his Family Theatre idea they were very skeptical of his chances of persuading any of the networks to put on the program, or that a religious program could ever garner a sufficiently large audience. But Father Peyton, instilled with the same determination and faith that had carried him through his project's early struggles, went straight to the program director of the Mutual Broadcasting System.

Reverend Patrick Peyton, founder of the Family Rosary Crusade.

"I have an idea for a new kind of radio program," Father Peyton started to explain and as he detailed the Family Rosary Crusade story for the station official, the same reaction that had prompted the Albany station official to grant the father's wishes appeared in this man's face. "I think it's a great idea, Father," the director said warmly, and he immediately began the arrangements for a trial broadcast.

The owner of an advertising agency also responded to the young priest's pleas by declaring, "I'll have a script written for your program's first broadcast and I'll be only too happy to shoulder all expenses." In New York City, Francis Cardinal Spellman heard of the plans for the program and quickly volunteered to appear on the first broadcast. The program director was amazed at Father Peyton's energy in obtaining so much help for his idea, and one day, merely as a joke, the director remarked to Father Peyton, "It's a wonder you haven't tried to get Bing Crosby." The father took the suggestion in dead earnest. He picked up the telephone, explained his mission to the operator, and, though he didn't personally know the celebrated popular singer, nor did Crosby know him, he was quickly put in touch with him in Hollywood. "I'll be proud to appear," Crosby said sincerely, "for Our Lady." The Blessed Sacrament Choir of New York and the parents of the five Sullivan boys who were lost at sea in World War II also agreed to appear, and a short time later the first trial broadcast went on the air.

The response to the experiment was so encouraging that on February 13, 1947, the first actual Family Theatre broadcast was given and the American radio audience quickly took to its heart this new kind of program, a program that was entertaining, but which also brought spiritual happiness into the homes of the listeners. The program's original fifty-station outlet has since grown to over four hundred and the Armed Forces Radio Service has added more than eighty-four more stations, all located outside the United States. Stars of show business as well as religious and political leaders gladly give of their time and effort to make each week's broadcast a memorable and inspirational event.

The Family Rosary Crusade has come far since 1941, but it is still growing. Father Peyton and his followers have carried the message of the Family Rosary to Canada, England, and Australia, and here in America to most of our states plus the District of Columbia and including faraway Alaska. The more than seven million pledges that have been obtained stand as a lasting fulfillment of Father Peyton's promise to God.

For a family wishing to gain the full benefit of the Rosary, Father Peyton has this suggestion: "All the members of the family, or as many as possible, gather together daily after the evening meal or at some other time. One of the group then recites the first part of the prayers and announces the mysteries. The others respond by reciting the last part of the prayers. The Apostles' Creed is said on the Crucifix, the Our Father on the large beads, the Hail Mary on the small beads, the Glory Be to the Father at the end of each group of small beads."

The ultimate success of the Family Rosary Crusade thus rests with the individual families who heed and practice what the Crusade envisions. As Father Peyton has said, "Peace and security can be gained for their own sacred homes by giving ten minutes out of every twenty-four hours to prayer."

# XXVII

# *Father Flanagan of Boys Town*

As HE WENT about his God-inspired work of helping homeless
and displaced human beings get a fresh start in life, Father
Edward Joseph Flanagan often found himself with few tangible financial resources to back his bold and noble ideas. But
this dedicated Roman Catholic priest, who would eventually
be revered by people of all religions, never let material matters
stand in the way of fulfilling his great humanitarian dreams.
He would simply say, "Faith is a kind of capital, too."

Faith was the driving force that sustained and uplifted this
servant of God and all mankind. Never discouraged or defeated
by the many setbacks and difficulties that continually plagued
him, unswerving and passionate in his desire to help improve
the lives of the underprivileged, Father Flanagan was to surmount every stumbling block and see his great dream of human
service reach a summit of achievement with his founding of
the now world-renowned Boys Town community in the
sprawling hills of Nebraska.

His own youth was a rich preparation for the great work
that would mark his adult years. He was born on July 13, 1886
on the fair-sized and steadily productive farm his parents main-

tained near the town of Ballymore in Ireland. The Flanagans were a large family. Eddie had eleven brothers and sisters, but his deeply religious parents imparted to all their children loving care and wise guidance.

Young Eddie was a small, frail child and he therefore had to be watched over very carefully. When he came of school age, he was enrolled at the nearby national school and proved himself a diligent student. He had a voracious appetite for learning. When not busy with his regular school work the youngster would often settle himself in a quiet spot and pore over some good books of his own to further widen his horizons of knowledge. One book especially fired the youngster's imagination, the Holy Bible. He read its ancient but ever new words of guidance and wisdom over and over. In this way the youngster developed the sense of high purpose to which he would dedicate his life.

At the age of fourteen young Eddie announced with calm sincerity to his family, "I want to become a priest."

No one in the Flanagan household opposed the youngster's fateful decision. "Eddie was born to be a priest," his parents said, and they knew that he would prove himself a credit to this highest calling of their religion.

Eddie launched his formal academic training at Summer Hill College in the Irish coast town of Sligo and graduated at the age of eighteen.

At about this time his sister Nora returned home from an extended visit to the United States. She spoke with great enthusiasm about the young, fast-growing land across the ocean. "Why don't you continue your studies for the priesthood in America?" she urged her brother.

Thus, in the year 1904, a tall, lean Irish lad joined the great wave of immigration to America's shores, an exodus that would bring to the new land the courageous and hard-working people whose talent and vision would contribute mightily to the growth and future greatness of the United States.

Soon after arriving in America, Eddie enrolled at Mount St. Mary's College in Emmitsburg, Maryland, where at the age of twenty he received his bachelor of arts degree.

He then went on to St. Joseph's Seminary in Dunwoodie, New York. Conscientiously applying himself to his studies, he also found time for volunteer work among the tubercular patients in several New York hospitals. "This world is full of careers for people who are willing to help," he commented with deep conviction. "Every hospital, every asylum, every orphan home is a want ad for a position with the Lord, doing His work. And the pay lies in helping to bring to someone a little moment brighter than the rest."

But he overworked himself and his frail body broke under the great strain. After a year at the Seminary he was forced to leave. His doctor confined him to his bed under strict orders to take it easy. But the self-sacrificing young man refused to let this setback stop him from pursuing his high ambition. "God gave me a purpose," he insisted, and he meant to fulfill this purpose no matter what the cost. So he arranged with the school to continue his studies at home, in this way he passed his examinations with high honors.

His strength slowly returned to his thin body and it was decided that he would probably regain his full health more quickly if he went to live in a warmer climate. He would journey west to Nebraska, where two of his brothers already resided, and settle in the city of Omaha, then still a very young but rapidly developing frontier town.

Friends advised him just to take an easy job and give up his physically taxing preparations for the priesthood, but Eddie was determined to carry through his great ambition. "I'm going to find the strength somehow," he insisted. "I am sure our dear Lord is going to help me."

As soon as his health appeared to be mended again, Eddie

The first five boys of Father Flanagan's Boys' Home.

The Boys Town woodworking shop.

set out for Rome to attend the Gregorian University. But a short while later his health again collapsed and he had to return to Omaha, still not a priest, but not defeated either by this setback to his glowing plans.

He took a job as an accountant at a local meat-packing concern, but his dream of some day reaching his high religious calling still dominated his thoughts. "I have faith that I shall be a priest," he declared with steadfast resolve.

And true to his faith in himself and in his desire to serve God by serving humanity, Eddie did a short while later enroll at the University of Innsbruck in Austria where, on the bright morning of July 26, 1912, he took his place with the other graduates as they walked down the aisle of St. Ignatius Church at Innsbruck in their glorious ordination procession.

Now it would be *Father* Flanagan who would return to Omaha. His first assignment would be as assistant priest at a church in the small Nebraska town of O'Neill but a little while later he would be transferred back to Omaha to serve as assistant priest at the city's St. Patrick's Church.

It was the summer of 1913, Omaha at that time was crowded with farm workers who, because of a blight in the crops that year, were now without work and roamed the streets of the city hungry and homeless. No one offered to help them. The young, idealistic priest was appalled by this shameful neglect of fellow human beings. He determined to do something himself to help these poor unfortunates.

With his own small salary and some money he was able to raise from friends, he purchased a good supply of food and distributed it to the workers.

Then he began to walk the streets of Omaha searching for some kind of dwelling that could provide at least temporary shelter for these homeless men. He came upon a battered and deserted two-story brick building. With a thorough sweeping and some repairs the place can be made livable, the young priest thought optimistically. He paid the first month's rent out of his own pocket, just about all the money he had in the world. His real capital, his unswerving faith, would have to carry him through all the difficulties and problems that lay ahead.

And God did provide. Friends and even total strangers heard of his work and gladly donated what they could to keep the Workingman's Hotel going. In a year he was able to move to better and larger quarters and to accommodate many more of the hungry and homeless of the city.

When he wasn't busy at the Hotel or taking care of his regular parish obligations, the young priest would often settle himself in a back row of Omaha's juvenile court. He would listen sadly as children were brought before the presiding judge, charged with some usually minor infraction of the law. They were children from broken homes or children without parents, youngsters who had never had the proper guidance that would have kept them out of trouble. Now they were being hustled off to so-called correctional institutions, from which, in a few years, they would almost certainly emerge as hardened and incorrigible criminals. What a senseless waste, the young priest thought angrily. And to anyone in the court who would listen to him Flanagan would say with passionate conviction, "Give these children a chance. Show them kindness and love instead of this cruel punishment, which gains nothing."

Finally, his heartfelt appeals touched the conscience of the presiding judge. "Very well, Father," the judge said to him one day. "I'll parole two of these boys into your care instead of sending them to the reformatory. Let's see if your way can really work."

Flanagan snatched at this opportunity to prove that his faith in youth was justified. He took the two boys completely under his wing. He would walk with them for hours, talking over their problems with them. He was never preachy or authoritarian with them. He was their friend, that was all. He talked to them about baseball and other healthy interests young boys shared, and he also spoke to them of God. Patiently and understandingly he explained to them how religious faith could help them lead constructive and purposeful lives. "You mustn't be afraid of God," he would say to them. "He's a loving Father. He understands how a boy can get into trouble sometimes."

His simple words of guidance and his sincere concern for their welfare convinced the boys that they should now conduct their lives in such a way that their friend Father Flanagan would be proud of them.

Soon more boys were being paroled into the young priest's care. He organized his young charges into a baseball club, again with confidence that his real capital, his faith, would provide the necessary equipment and operating funds. And they *were* provided, by the many well-wishers who came forward to donate the money and materials he needed.

But it soon became apparent to young Father Flanagan that if his guidance and help were to have a lasting effect on the youngsters, and if he was to help the many other homeless and underprivileged boys of the city, he had first to find a place where the boys could live and study. His superior, Archbishop Harty, of Omaha, heartily endorsed his idea, but he had to add reluctantly that because his office operated on very limited funds he could not give him any financial assistance with his hopeful venture. "You will have to look only and entirely to your own resources," he told him.

In the days to follow, the young priest would have to summon all his faith to carry him through, his faith in God and his faith that there were other people who believed as he did in the potential for good inherent in all young boys.

He found a two-story red-brick building that he felt would make an ideal haven for homeless, neglected, and underprivi-

Rt. Rev. Msgr. Edward J. Flanagan,
founder of Boys Town.

*Walter S. Craig*

Rt. Rev. Msgr. Nicholas H. Wegner,
director of Boys Town.

leged boys. But the rent was ninety dollars a month and at the moment he had less then ninety cents of his own. But a friend heard of his plight, and lent him the money to pay the first month's rent. On December 10, 1917, Father Flanagan's first Boy's Home officially opened its doors, its arms of welcome extended for any boy in need of food, shelter and, perhaps most of all, guidance and love.

He began with just five youngsters, but this soon climbed to twenty-five. They were boys of all religions and all races, all God's children. When a prejudiced Omaha resident criticized him for having white, Chinese, and Negro children together at the Home, Father Flanagan replied simply, "And could you please tell me what is the color of the soul?"

His superiors were deeply impressed by his accomplishments and he was relieved of all his other obligations. By September, 1921, the young priest had already helped many needy boys, but there were still many more who clamored to live at the Home, including boys from other states. However, space in the small building was now at a critical premium.

It was then that the young priest recalled a beautiful piece of farmland he had once seen located some ten miles west of Omaha. It was rich, productive land but no one was using it. Why should this good land just go to waste when my boys could put it to such good use? Father Flanagan thought to himself. The vision came to him of building an actual town here, where poor boys could live and study and work, all in a healthy, invigorating country atmosphere. They would stay in "Boys Town" until they reached young manhood and were ready to take their place in society as physically and spiritually mature adults.

But the cost of the 160-acre tract of land was several thousand dollars. All Flanagan had at the time was a small bank account and some forty acres of second-rate farmland that he had purchased with the financial aid of friends a short while before as a possible camping site for his boys. Would this be enough to secure the good farmland?

He went to the owner of the property, a very successful Omaha businessman named David Baum, and poured out to him his glorious ideas. It would be a great investment, the priest insisted, an investment in our youth, the future of America.

"You want me to take a business gamble on an experiment with a crop of bad boys?" Baum replied sharply.

"Mr. Baum, there are no bad boys," Flanagan answered with deep conviction. "How can they be? They are just children—God's children." (In years to come the heartfelt expression "There are no bad boys," which Flanagan first uttered that day, would become the great rallying cry of his entire humanitarian movement.)

Baum gave the young priest's words considerable thought. By all the accepted rules of business this was certainly a bad investment, he realized. The priest had no really tangible assets to speak of, and if the idea failed it would be Baum who would be blamed for the financial loss. Yet the usually hardheaded businessman was also deeply moved by the humble, unswerving confidence of the young priest. "Your greatest business asset seems to be your faith," Baum said with an admiring smile. And he too would have faith, faith in this dedicated priest and faith in youth, the good and useful citizens of tomorrow.

"Surely such a noble idea should at least be given a chance," Baum declared. "I will take the forty acres as the down-payment on the land. You keep what cash you have in the bank. You will need it to pay for the building of living quarters and so forth for your boys. You can pay me the balance of the cost of the land in installments when you have the money."

Thus, on October 17, 1921, Boys Town was born. "It will not be a prison," Father Flanagan immediately stated. "It will be a home." There would be no gates, no locks, and no fences anywhere in the unique community. Any boy could leave whenever he wished to do so. No one would stop them. For those who did choose to stay, Flanagan set down only one hard and fast rule of conduct. They must attend religious services at least once a week and such services would be provided for every faith.

And the boys did come, and did stay. They arrived by bus, by train, and on foot from just about every state in the Union. Some trudged many miles until they reached the top of the hill and looked down on the sun-baked Nebraska fields that told them they were at Boys Town—they were home.

A citizens' committee of adults of all religions was formed to carry on fund-raising campaigns that would enable the community to continue to grow and prosper. From the first, it was decided that the boys' community would be supported solely by the good-will offerings of private citizens, and not by any governmental or religious agency. Thus, Boys Town would always belong to all the people and be a continuous expression of humanity's deep concern for its youth.

In March, 1922, a gleaming new main building was erected on the site, and in 1927 the Boys Town Trade School was established. Here the boys could supplement the grade school through high school academic education they were already receiving by learning such skills as woodworking, baking, barbering, the printing trades, electronics, and others so that when they left Boys Town they would have little difficulty obtaining a job and assuming the obligations and responsibilities of adulthood.

Boys Town is run for and by its young residents. The youngsters govern the community themselves by electing their own mayor, councilmen, and commissioners, all boys themselves, and by seeing to it that the town is always operating on an even keel.

Walter S. Craig

Father Flanagan and the Boys Town Choir.

Sports are probably the town's biggest spare-time activity. In addition, in 1941 Father Flanagan organized a fifty-voice Boys Town Choir, which is today one of the most famous and outstanding of such groups in the world.

In the spring of 1948, while traveling in Europe to study and help improve overseas child-welfare programs, Father Flanagan, then 62, suddenly succumbed to a heart ailment. He died peacefully and his body was returned to his beloved Boys Town for burial in the chapel so that he would always be within hearing of the joyful and healthy laughter of his boys.

Today, under the equally dedicated direction of his successor, Monsignor Nicholas H. Wegner, Boys Town continues to function for the greater glory of God and humanity. The community now stretches over some 1,500 acres and encloses more than fifty imposing buildings.

Thousands of boys have called Boys Town their home at one time or another. The encouragement and proper guidance they received enabled them to start off on the right footing and today they are among our nation's most prominent and exemplary citizens.

The farm boy from Ireland, frail in body but imbued with great strength of character, had brought it all about and with little else but his own "real capital," his indomitable faith in God, in himself as an instrument of God's work, and in youth. From this great wellspring of his faith flowed all the heralded achievements that crowned Father Edward Flanagan's lifetime of service to humanity.